American Military History

A Captivating Guide to Events and Facts You Should Know About Armed Conflicts Involving the United States

© Copyright 2023 - All rights reserved.

The content contained within this book may not be reproduced, duplicated, or transmitted without direct written permission from the author or the publisher.

Under no circumstances will any blame or legal responsibility be held against the publisher, or author, for any damages, reparation, or monetary loss due to the information contained within this book, either directly or indirectly.

Legal Notice:

This book is copyright protected. It is only for personal use. You cannot amend, distribute, sell, use, quote, or paraphrase any part, or the content within this book, without the consent of the author or publisher.

Disclaimer Notice:

Please note the information contained within this document is for educational and entertainment purposes only. All effort has been executed to present accurate, up-to-date, reliable, and complete information. No warranties of any kind are declared or implied. Readers acknowledge that the author is not engaging in the rendering of legal, financial, medical, or professional advice. The content within this book has been derived from various sources. Please consult a licensed professional before attempting any techniques outlined in this book.

By reading this document, the reader agrees that under no circumstances is the author responsible for any losses, direct or indirect, that are incurred as a result of the use of the information contained within this document, including, but not limited to, errors, omissions, or inaccuracies.

Free Bonus from Captivating History (Available for a Limited time)

Hi History Lovers!

Now you have a chance to join our exclusive history list so you can get your first history ebook for free as well as discounts and a potential to get more history books for free! Simply visit the link below to join.

Captivatinghistory.com/ebook

Also, make sure to follow us on Facebook, Twitter and Youtube by searching for Captivating History.

Table of Contents

INTRODUCTION: THE BEGINNING OF IT ALL 1
PART ONE: THE COLONIAL AND REVOLUTIONARY PERIOD (1689–1783) 3
CHAPTER 1: QUEEN ANNE'S WAR AND THE FRENCH AND INDIAN WAR 4
CHAPTER 2: THE AMERICAN REVOLUTION 11
PART TWO: FROM REVOLUTION TO CIVIL WAR (1783–1865) 24
CHAPTER 3: THE EARLY NATIONAL PERIOD (1783–1812) AND THE WAR OF 1812 25
CHAPTER 4: THE TEXAS REVOLUTION AND THE MEXICAN-AMERICAN WAR 31
CHAPTER 5: THE AMERICAN CIVIL WAR 37
PART THREE: FROM THE END OF THE CIVIL WAR TO WWI (1865–1918) 44
CHAPTER 6: THE AMERICAN INDIAN WARS (1865–1891) 45
CHAPTER 7: THE SPANISH-AMERICAN AND THE PHILIPPINE WARS (1898–1902) 52
CHAPTER 8: THE USA JOINS WWI (1917–1918) 59
PART FOUR: FROM WWII TO THE WAR ON TERROR (1941–2019) 68
CHAPTER 9: WWII: BECOMING A SUPERPOWER 69
CHAPTER 10: POST-WAR REFORMATIONS 76
CHAPTER 11: THE COLD WAR CHALLENGES (1945–1990) 79

CHAPTER 12: POST-COLD WAR (1990-2001) AND THE
21ST CENTURY (2001-2021) CONFLICTS 90
CONCLUSION: THE VIEW FROM THE TOP 94
HERE'S ANOTHER BOOK BY CAPTIVATING HISTORY
THAT YOU MIGHT LIKE 96
FREE BONUS FROM CAPTIVATING HISTORY
(AVAILABLE FOR A LIMITED TIME) 97
APPENDIX A: FURTHER READING AND REFERENCE 98

Introduction: The Beginning of It All

The American military had some rather humble beginnings, but it would ultimately evolve into the greatest fighting force the world has ever known. In some ways, such words might sound like hyperbole, but when one considers the power of the United States, one can't help but realize the impactful role the US military plays in that.

The might of the US military is not so much reflected by massive conquests and military triumphs, which was the case of the mighty military powers of old. The Romans, Spanish, British, and other "Old World" powers typically showed their might with empire-building conquests. But that was not the case with the United States.

For the most part, the military power of the United States is demonstrated by its effect of deterrence. If one doubts the power of the United States to restrain the aggression of other nations, just consider for a moment what the world might be like if the United States military was not in the equation.

If it weren't for the restraining power of the United States, China wouldn't hesitate to invade Taiwan. North Korea would run roughshod on South Korea. Iran would destroy Israel (or at least try its best to), and countless would-be conquerors would bully their neighbors all over the globe. The policing power of the United States makes any would-be aggressor think twice.

One might point to Russia's 2022 invasion of Ukraine and say, "Well, so much for that!" But if we examine even the Russia/Ukraine conflict closer, we realize that the restraining power of the US military is there as well. As bad as the Russian invasion of Ukraine has been, without the threat of direct military action by the United States, it would be even worse.

Without the United States, what would stop Russia from unleashing its full fury on Ukraine? Vladimir Putin's invasion was brutal, but he did show some restraint. Without the threat of the US military, Putin may well have turned Ukraine's cities into nuclear infernos.

So, yes, even though the US military does not go around conquering the world, the power of the US as a deterrent manages to keep the status quo of the world together in a way that could be described as the "Pax Americana."

The Roman peace, or the "Pax Romana," was done through outright conquest of any rival. But the Pax Americana has been achieved by the mere threat of action if anyone disrupts international norms. So far, this is the legacy of the American military in the world today and a growing theme that we will explore further throughout this book.

PART ONE: THE COLONIAL AND REVOLUTIONARY PERIOD (1689–1783)

Chapter 1: Queen Anne's War and the French and Indian War

"Soldiers, when committed to a task, can't compromise. It's unrelenting devotion to the standards of duty and courage, absolute loyalty to others, not letting the task go until it's been done."

-John Keegan

It's important to examine the American military's colonial roots prior to the establishment of the United States. The colonial armies, which were under British administration, were the immediate forerunners of what would become the fully fledged independent US Armed Forces. And one of the first major conflicts to involve the colonial forces of America was Queen Anne's War.

This war was an ongoing conflict between Britain, France, and Spain. The war was called such because the reigning British monarch of the time was Queen Anne. And since the American colonies belonged to Britain, it makes sense that the American colonial forces were mobilized to fight this war on behalf of Queen Anne.

The hostilities first erupted in the year 1701 with the ill-fated War of the Spanish Succession, which was waged in Europe after the passing of the Spanish monarch, King Charles II. Soon, hostilities erupted in North America, with Spanish-controlled Florida skirmishing with the nearby British-controlled colony then known as the Province of Carolina.

The north was a theater of war between the British colony of New England on the northeast coast and French holdings in Acadia, Quebec, and Newfoundland. The war really took off when French and British colonists began to engage in hostilities over their respective hegemony over the Mississippi River. These intrigues led to both the British and the French forging various alliances with local Native American tribes in an effort to offset their adversaries.

There were not too many heavily fortified locations in these early years, save perhaps for some well-developed outposts like the Spanish town of St. Augustine or the British port of New York. For the most part, much of America was still in an underdeveloped state. The nation was a sprawling rural landscape pocketed with thick wilderness areas.

Unlike the state parks of today, these pristine environments, as beautiful as they were, were not the kind of places where one should walk alone. The second anyone went off the beaten path, they were in a vast "no man's land" where just about anything could happen. Most of the military forts—if you could even call them as such—were essentially wooden stockades that made hearty use of the trees they were surrounded by.

These structures were essentially walled-in towns, somewhat similar to a medieval castle, except not extravagant and minus the drawbridge. Inside these forts were plots of land for food, which was grown to sustain the people living there. There was always someone on guard at the watchtower to ensure that no one would get the drop on those inside the fort.

It was from these rustic, wooden forts that the first command posts of what would become the American military were derived. The American military was, of course, based on the British military. The colonials, just like their counterparts in mainland Britain, found it conducive to break up their armed forces into small but highly effective militias. And these militias largely waged Queen Anne's War in North America.

Although these colonial forces were equipped with the latest muskets and artillery, they also utilized weapons that would be considered "throwbacks" to a more distant period. Militias usually wielded pikes, which were not particularly dissimilar from those used during the Middle Ages. Pikes are somewhat similar to a knight's javelin. They are long wooden poles with steel tips attached to them.

The colonial forces faced an onslaught of French troops on August 10th, 1703, in what was known as the Northeast Coast campaign. This was the first major French offensive against the British colonists in New England. The French forces were comprised of some five hundred French and Native American troops, and they stormed several colonial settlements up and down the northeast coast. Settlements were destroyed, and over 150 people died or were taken prisoner.

Even so, the English forces would rally, and the French would soon come out on the losing end. Queen Anne's War ultimately came to an end with the signing of the Treaty of Utrecht. This treaty also brought the War of the Spanish Succession to a conclusion. By the terms of this treaty, the British gained Acadia from the French, which the British subsequently renamed Nova Scotia. The British also secured sovereignty over Newfoundland and their hegemony over the entire Hudson Bay. The French would also cough up New Brunswick and what today constitutes the easternmost portion of the state of Maine.

Queen Anne's War was fairly far-reaching. But the Seven Years' War was a truly global conflict that had the major European powers duking it out in Europe, as well as in their colonial possessions. The North American theater of this war is often dubbed the French and Indian War. It was named as such because American colonial troops battled against both the French and their Native American (Indian) allies. The colonists also had help from Native American allies as well.

But even though the French and Indian War often gets lumped in with the Seven Years' War, it is important to note that the French and Indian War actually erupted a couple of years prior to the start of the Seven Years' War. The Seven Years' War is said to have begun in 1756, whereas the French and Indian War can be traced back to 1754.

And the North American theater of what would later become a truly global conflict first saw increased hostilities when none other than future President George Washington, who was only twenty-two at the time, oversaw a joint British and Native American force that devastated French troops during the Battle of Jumonville Glen. This battle occurred on May 28th, 1754.

The whole ordeal began over a minor territorial dispute over whether or not the British had the right to build a fortress in what is now Pittsburgh, Pennsylvania. The French claimed this particular piece of real estate as theirs, yet the British were intent on building their fortifications in the disputed region. Before the outbreak of hostilities, French troops had driven off a small group of British forces who were building the fort.

Washington and his men were sent to confront the aggressive French troops. They were able to ambush a group of French Canadians led by Joseph Coulon de Jumonville. During the course of the battle, Jumonville was killed, and most of his troops were taken prisoner. What was a minor incident over what should have been a minor territorial dispute ignited the French and Indian War and ultimately paved the way for even further conflict. The French said that Jumonville was a diplomat looking to deliver a message to the British; the British said he was a spy. Historians still aren't sure if Jumonville was actually acting as a diplomat or not, but the French back then took great offense to his death.

One of Washington's own contemporaries, Horace Walpole, stated that "the volley fired by a young Virginian in the backwoods of America set the world on fire."

The Seven Years' War would kick off in 1756 in Europe theatre. The nation of Prussia was bitterly fighting the Austrians in a bid to influence the trajectory of the Holy Roman Empire. The Holy Roman Empire was a conglomeration of states in western and central Europe that had existed (off and on) since the time of Charlemagne. The conflict between Austria and Prussia erupted over the fate of a small slice of land called Silesia.

Silesia, which is now part of Poland, was heavily contested by the powers of Prussia and Austria. Just as the borders of nations have expanded and shrunk over time, it is also important to note that some nations no longer exist, as is the case with Prussia. Prussia was once part of the Holy Roman Empire but was declared an independent kingdom in 1701. Prussia, which included a large chunk of Poland and much of what we now call Germany, was the forerunner to the modern German state and was incorporated into the German Empire in 1871.

At any rate, as it pertains to the Seven Years' War, things really heated up when Britain switched sides in the struggle, joining forces with Prussia and taking the fight directly to France and Austria. Prussia decided to launch a preemptive attack on the principality of Saxony. The attack was a success, and Saxony was defeated, but it created a tremendous backlash against the Prussians.

Spain chose to side with France and, with French support, launched an invasion of Portugal in 1762. Portugal was in the throes of a populist government known as the Pombaline dictatorship. The Spanish and French invasion was ultimately checked by a popular uprising of the people. However, the Spaniards would gain more ground in South America, waging battles against the Portuguese holdings in Brazil. Ultimately, it was a losing battle for Spain.

The French in North America did much better, scoring some early victories with their Native American allies. Perhaps the most damaging loss to the British was when their star general, General Edward Braddock, saw his army almost completely annihilated. The Battle of Monongahela occurred on July 9th, 1755, near the Monongahela River, near today's city of Pittsburgh.

Braddock's contingent was waylaid by a force of French bolstered by their Native American allies, and it was entirely overwhelmed. A disorderly retreat of British forces ensued in which Braddock himself was shot in the chest. His wounds would prove fatal, and he would ultimately perish from his injuries a few days later, on July 13th, 1755.

However, even when the British scored victories, it was often a mixed bag, as had happened in 1759. On September 13th, 1759, Wolfe and a group of some 4,400 British troops made landfall in Quebec, just off the banks of the St. Lawrence River.

These daring soldiers then climbed up a steep incline and were able to literally get the drop on French positions below. Pummeled by cannons, the French were forced out into the open, where a terrible battle ensued. The French were ultimately defeated, but just as victory was theirs, Wolfe was hit multiple times, receiving wounds in his shoulder, arm, and chest. The great General Wolfe, who had engineered this stunning victory, perished moments later on the Plains of Abraham.

The British were perhaps the harshest on their failed generals. They famously executed their own Admiral John Byng after he was court-martialed for supposedly "failing to do his utmost" during a French attack. Nevertheless, both France and Spain would come out as the losers of the Seven Years' War and would lose large tracts of land as a consequence.

France lost much of its territory in Canada, and Spain lost Florida and territory along the Gulf Coast. Britain's triumph in the Seven Years' War (and the French and Indian War by extension) allowed the nation to become a truly global empire. The war devastated Britain's rivals and increased its territory. The war also boosted Britain's navy, allowing the country to create a formidable naval force that would travel the globe.

However, this new empire would bring with it many changes. The British now had more territories to control in North America thanks to the territory gained in Canada, which was officially seized after the 1763 Treaty of Paris. This meant there had to be a large occupation force stationed in the region that would consume considerable resources.

In order to recoup the losses from the war, taxes had to be raised in the colonies. And as anyone who has ever heard the pre-revolutionary slogan "no taxation without representation" knows, these arbitrary (at least arbitrary from the perspective of the colonists) tax hikes would light the spark for an all-out revolution. That famous phrase echoes the complaint that the faraway British Parliament was expecting these changes in the tax code, not local assemblies. And yes, the colonies did indeed have their own local assemblies. The problem was the British Parliament could easily override them.

Perhaps the most influential city in the growing rebellion was Boston. There were many protests and revolts in the city, and the British had to send in large numbers of troops just to keep an eye on things. This set the stage for what would become known as the Boston Massacre, when British soldiers opened fire on colonial protesters on March 5th, 1770.

The massacre started after protesters began heckling soldiers. One thing led to another, and soon the British soldiers were firing into the hostile crowd. All in all, about five people were killed, and several others were wounded.

However, the damage to the reputation of British authorities was even worse, and the sternest of taskmasters realized that the Boston

Massacre had done them no good. In a show of remorse, the British removed troops. This did calm the waters for a while, but by 1773, the situation would erupt once the Intolerable Acts were passed.

Chapter 2: The American Revolution

"The army as usual is without pay, and a great part of the soldiery without shirts; and tho' the patience of them is equally threadbare, it seems to be a matter of small concern to those at a distance. In truth, if one was to hazard an opinion for them on this subject, it would be that the army, having contracted a habit of encountering distress and difficulties and of living without money, it would be injurious to it to introduce other customs."

-George Washington

It could be rightly said that the United States of America was forged in the fires of war. After all, the nascent colonial armed forces of America had to fight a war in order to shake off British authority. It has been said that the American Revolution was a time that tested and tempered the entire American mentality of war.

The hopes and expectations of the Patriots who struggled against their British overlords were perhaps a bit extravagant and grandiose considering the circumstances. These meager militias were challenging what was, at that time, the greatest maritime empire on the planet. The sun might never have set on the British Empire, but these colonial Patriots were more than determined to create a new dawn for themselves regardless.

The idea that the people could be free from their perceived tyranny was a popular and optimistic strain of thought. And the people latched onto this hope, leading them to believe they would win the day against the British. From the beginning of the struggle, it was determined that fighting men should be pulled from every segment of society through the use of volunteers from local militias.

The Patriots believed that a standing army fighting merely for pay would not have the same fighting spirit and passion as local community volunteers. People who believed in the cause would fight as hard as they could because their moral convictions told them their cause was right and that it was worth fighting and dying for. Leading the call were many philosophers and thinkers, such as Thomas Paine, whose pamphlet on individual freedoms called *Common Sense* became one of the go-to pieces of literature (perhaps propaganda is a better word) for the continental armed forces of the Americans.

Back in the early days of 1775, several cities in and around Boston began the steady lurch toward war. Boston was often the political epicenter of the general discontent that the colonists felt. It was in Boston that protesters were massacred, and it was in Boston that Patriots, incensed at the Tea Act that gave the British East India Company a monopoly on selling tea to the colonies, infamously dumped a bunch of tea overboard in what was eventually dubbed the Boston Tea Party. The Tea Act was just the match that lit the fire, as tensions had been building for some time.

This event took place on the night of December 16th, 1773, and involved protestors resorting to what was basically a brazen attack. Americans may like to look back at the Boston Tea Party today with nostalgia, but when considering what actually happened, it is easy to understand why the British might have been a little miffed.

For those who are unaware of the events of the Boston Tea Party, a group of colonists decided they would dress up as Native Americans, jump on board a boat docked in the harbor, and break open chest after chest of tea leaves, only to dump their contents into the water. This was no small feat since tea leaves were an expensive commodity. The incident resulted in a considerable amount of money being squandered and the nerves of merchants being severely frayed.

King George III was greatly incensed at what had happened and took special offense to the Boston Tea Party. After this infamous event, British Parliament shut down Boston's port, declaring that it would remain closed until the local Bostonians were able to provide enough recompense to have it reopened.

Other Intolerable Acts were passed, most of which targeted Massachusetts. But instead of teaching the Bostonians a lesson, such actions only served to radicalize them even more. Many Americans had grown resentful of what they viewed as British overreach. Even the Quebec Act of 1774 became a major point of contention since it was viewed as the British arbitrarily granting favoritism to the less-populated region of Quebec over the much more populous and established settlements of the northeastern seaboard.

Americans also watched as much of the Ohio Country was incorporated into Quebec. The Ohio Country was a large tract of unsettled territory that was made up of parts of modern-day West Virginia, Pennsylvania, Ohio, and Indiana. The American colonists were deeply suspicious of the French settlers in Quebec, and the Protestants were leery of French Catholic expansion.

The fact that the region would be administered by a Crown-appointed governor without a legislative assembly also stoked fears among the American colonists that the colonies would be based on that same model. They feared that they would lose their assemblies and have a British-backed governor foisted upon them.

Arms were stocked up seemingly on every corner, and there were routine calls for folks to join local militias. In light of all this preparedness, it is a bit surprising how off-guard the American Patriots were when the British forces finally came calling.

King George III had been kept abreast of what was happening, and he ordered that all of Massachusetts be considered to be in a state of rebellion. He then sent General Thomas Gage into the region to seek out hidden weapons caches so that the arms could be collected and removed from the Patriots.

On April 18th, 1775, a large contingent of British troops landed in Massachusetts. Shortly thereafter, militia members holed up in nearby Buckman Tavern. Led by Captain John Parker, this group stood out like a sore thumb. After Parker gave them their marching orders, they assembled into two companies and headed to the Lexington Common. There, they collided with a large contingent of British troops, which had arrived to disarm the colonists. It seemed as if the colonial militia didn't stand much of a chance.

History remains muted as to who fired the first shot during what would become the Battle of Lexington/Concord, but the British would always claim that they tried to exercise restraint. Their orders were to take weapons caches and disband rebel groups, not to engage in wanton bloody battles. And it's said that upon approaching the tavern, the captain of this British contingent, Lieutenant John Pitcairn, made this objective entirely clear.

He is recorded to have given a direct order, stating, "Soldiers, don't fire! Keep your ranks. Form and surround them." His fellow officers were then said to have been heard shouting, "Throw down your arms, you villains! You rebels! Disperse immediately!" If this had happened, then war might have been averted that day. But such things weren't meant to be.

Instead, at some point, a shot was fired. The shot could have been from a British soldier, or it could have been from one of the American revolutionary fighters; historians still aren't clear on this. But this one shot would lead to a terrific fight the morning of April 19th and ultimately ignited the Revolutionary War in earnest.

Once the British guns began firing in earnest, the militiamen rallied and struck back at the British as they headed over to conduct searches for weapons caches in Concord. In this skirmish, some 250 British troops were killed or wounded, whereas only about ninety American colonists are said to have perished or been wounded.

The American militias regrouped and headed for Boston. Boston had been taken over by British forces, and in line with King George III's instructions, citizens were being forcibly disarmed.

If anyone ever wonders why the Second Amendment right to bear arms is so ingrained in the American fabric, just picture the British forcibly disarming Americans. Such things were certainly front and center in the minds of those who drafted the Constitution.

By the end of that April, it is estimated about 1,778 firelocks, 634 pistols, 973 bayonets, and 38 blunderbusses (guns that were considered antique relics of the past even back then) were captured. The British were in control at this point. But even so, the British only had what amounted to a small respite, for these occupiers of Boston would ultimately become besieged.

The Battle of Bunker Hill took place on June 17th, 1775, in the vicinity of Charlestown, Massachusetts. Here, the British forces found themselves surrounded and decidedly outnumbered. Although they would prevail in the end, the British took that hill while suffering twice as many casualties as the Americans. Charlestown ended up being burned to the ground, and the death toll among the British defenders did not seem to justify the incinerated terrain that they had gained.

These developments were more than welcomed by the revolutionary troops, which were seeking to inflict as much pain on the British as possible. As General Nathaniel Greene put it at the time, "I wish [we] could sell them another hill at the same price."

Greene speculated that if every single engagement was won by the British with such a tremendous "price" in British blood, it would become unsustainable for the British. Even with Great Britain's tremendous resources, it could not afford to send men and equipment into a perpetual meat grinder, especially considering the massive need for troops in other parts of the British Empire. The goal of the revolutionaries was not the complete defeat of the British Empire but rather to sap its will to fight and agree to give the colonies their independence.

All the colonists had to do was hold on long enough and become enough of a burden on the British forces to ensure the war would be called off. The Americans had good reason to believe as much since there were many in British Parliament who wanted nothing to do with this conflict. These politicians disdainfully referred to it as a "fratricidal war" of brother against brother. Probably one of the greatest and most outspoken critics of the war was British philosopher Edmund Burke, who famously petitioned the House of Commons to end the conflict.

In the meantime, the Americans sought to replenish their lacking stores by stealing from the British. Interestingly enough, an order went out that any man who was able to retrieve a British cannonball from the battlefield would be monetarily rewarded. Considering how poor some of the members of these militias were, the notion of financial gain was so incentivizing that it could not be resisted. And as soon as a cannonball fell, there were often eager militiamen running toward it to claim it for a reward.

As inventive as this strategy was, it ultimately had to be rescinded when the competition among militiamen to retrieve cannonballs became too dangerous. It was said that some militiamen were actually losing their feet by trying to chase down cannonballs still in motion. Even so, the eagerness of these American militiamen and their desire to overcome their struggles (in this case, a lack of money) is a fairly good portrait of the struggle that Americans faced.

These ragtag colonists were up against the greatest, richest power on the planet, and all that kept them going was their own passion and unbridled spirit to not give in to defeat. It also didn't hurt that they had the home advantage. The British were far from home, but the Americans were right in their own backyard. They were able to take full advantage of the terrain and made good use of ambushes and other guerilla warfare tactics.

The colonists routinely faced low supplies. At one point, an inquiry revealed that much of the meat the militiamen ate was composed more of horse than beef. Despite the lack of resources, once the militias gained the upper hand, wide-scale looting and pillaging were expressly forbidden.

The officers did their best to rein in any aggressive impulses and to keep the men from exploiting others at the barrel of a gun. The revolutionaries had often criticized the British as being overbearing tyrants, so it would be unseemly for them to battle tyranny only to engage in acts of it themselves. To keep their ranks from getting too unruly and out of hand, military officers demanded that their troops stay orderly and punished any infractions that were committed. An indication of this strict discipline was recorded in the later recollection of Simon Fobes, who took part in the effort.

Fobes would later recall, "While we lay at Dorchester, the non-commissioned officers and privates of our company agreed upon some by-laws, to be in force among ourselves, particularly with regard to pilfering and uncleanliness about the camp. If anyone, on being accused and tried by a court-martial consisting of the sergeants of the company, was found guilty, he was fined or whipped at the discretion of the court. These by-laws were strictly enforced. A soldier was brought before the court for some misdemeanor, tried, found guilty, and sentenced to be whipped. He was immediately taken into an orchard, tied to an apple-tree and smartly whipped with rods. Another was caught on a pear-tree stealing fruit, and he was tried and severely punished."

Order was needed to keep the united front of the militias from falling apart. The leading general of this conflict, George Washington, seemed to personally share this view. After the terrible defeat that his forces suffered at Kip's Bay on September 15th, 1776, Washington weighed in on the matter. Washington spoke of the men under his command in some rather blunt terms when he wrote to his cousin, Lund Washington.

The letter read in part, "[The New England militia] are by no means such troops, in any respect, as you are led to believe of them from the accounts which are published, but I need not make myself enemies among them; by this declaration, although it is consistent with the truth. I daresay the men fight very well (if properly officered) although they are exceedingly dirty and nasty people."

We may perhaps forgive this future first US president's bluntness in his critique of his own men in consideration of what they were up against and what Washington had to work with. Washington's militia was full of colonists who had just been recruited right out of their villages. Many were uneducated, and most had no military training.

It's not too surprising then that Washington, who formerly served with the British military in highly refined and disciplined military units, was appalled at what he saw as a highly unprofessional army. Perhaps he even saw them as a slovenly group of wannabee soldiers in comparison to the British. He knew the men under his charge had the desire to fight, but he believed they needed to be molded into a disciplined fighting force in order to truly be useful in the war.

Just prior to the events at Kip's Bay in the meantime, the revolutionaries had been looking to continue their momentum by striking out at nearby Quebec City in December of 1775. American General Richard Montgomery famously stated that they would all either "eat Christmas dinner in Quebec City or in hell." As a general note to anyone who makes declarative statements like this, it usually serves no good and only jinxes everyone. Perhaps it's best not to use them!

After attempts were made to take the heavily fortified Quebec City, Washington's troops were repulsed. This attack on Quebec City is noteworthy because it was led by none other than the infamous

Benedict Arnold. For those who don't know, Arnold would go down in history as one of the greatest traitors of all time when he switched sides and joined the British.

But during the siege of Quebec City, Benedict Arnold was all in for the Americans. Montgomery, who had declared that he would be in "Quebec City or hell" by Christmas, was made into mincemeat from a hail of bullets, and Benedict Arnold took charge. Arnold was grievously injured in the leg but fought on regardless. Arnold attempted to lead a siege against the city, but by the spring of 1776, when British reinforcements were imminent, the whole botched endeavor had to be called off.

The British, in the meantime, were preparing to mobilize for an all-out war. Before, they had believed this was a small rebellion that could be easily put down, but things had changed. Massive troop drives were established, and even foreign mercenaries from German principalities, who would be dubbed the Hessians, were recruited for the cause. But no matter how many troops and resources the British threw at their problem, their biggest obstacle would remain logistics.

Even though the Thirteen Colonies sat along the East Coast, the coastline was a daunting challenge for the British navy. The coastline stretched some 1,500 miles, and due to the nature of the American colonies at the time, there was no major capital to destroy. The colonies were a confederation of semi-autonomous regions working in collaboration with each other.

The British essentially found themselves fighting a many-headed serpent. As soon as they cut off one head, another would pop up. Considering as much, it is perhaps no coincidence that one of the popular slogans of the Americans was "Don't tread on me," which features none other than a snake representing the Thirteen Colonies! Considering how proud the Americans were of this feat, it is a wonder that the national mascot did not end up being a snake instead of an eagle.

Because of these logistical problems, the British strategy revolved around securing a launching pad in New York, which could then be used to strike out at American forces.

Washington and his troops would rally, and soon he had them in prime fighting shape. These brave men fought in frigid cold conditions, famously culminating in the Christmas crossing of the

Delaware River in the year 1776.

The crossing was meant to enable an assault on the positions of the British auxiliary forces, the Hessians. These auxiliaries were crucial to British operations in Trenton, New Jersey. The Hessians were tough, battle-hardened troops, but they were not expecting the colonists to cross over the Delaware in the dead of night. If anything, they were looking toward the eastern seaboard for the threat of a naval attack. An attack by land was not even considered.

Washington's successful crossing of the Delaware gave him and his forces a tremendous advantage. The British high command was basically ready to quarter for the winter, take time to recoup, and consider the upcoming spring strategy. They most certainly were not expecting to have to fend off a major attack launched across the waters of the Delaware.

Washington knew the crossing would be difficult and pose a major hardship on his tired and weary soldiers, but he also knew that to seize the initiative, a great sacrifice would have to be made. As planning for the crossing was underway, a frequent mouthpiece of the revolution, Thomas Paine, penned a piece called *The American Crisis*. Paine was speaking in generalities about the revolution, but the words stirred Washington's heart keenly in regard to the upcoming crossing of the Delaware.

He felt the words related well enough to their situation, and he encouraged all of his troops to read the pamphlet and be inspired by it. The prose that so inspired him was the following:

"These are the times that try men's souls: The summer soldier and the sunshine patriot will, in this crisis, shrink from the service of his country; but he that stands it now, deserves the love and thanks of man and woman. Tyranny, like hell, is not easily conquered; yet we have this consolation with us, that the harder the conflict, the more glorious the triumph."

As Washington and his troops stood before the Delaware River later that day, it was indeed the kind of time that "tried men's souls." The water was not only freezing cold, but a winter storm erupted, with terrible winds whipping the troops in the face and cutting through them like ice-cold razor blades. There was also an icy mix of snow and rain pummeling them, bringing with it the prospect of frostbite and pneumonia if they were to linger for long.

Yet once they stood across the banks of the Delaware River, they knew they had reached the point of no return. There would be no going back. Men, their horses, and even large pieces of artillery were moved across the river. Everyone depended upon Washington and the half-frozen river to hold up long enough for them to safely cross to the other side.

The British and their Hessian auxiliaries had been lulled into a false sense of security. They engaged in elaborate Christmas celebrations the night before. British officers were said to have been stuffing themselves, drinking, and making merry. Commanding officer Colonel Johann Rall was at the house of a Loyalist named Abraham Hunt, where he and his cohorts stayed up late, taking in as much of the Christmas festivities as they could. They were likely ready to sleep in, totally unaware that Washington and his forces were planning to cross the Delaware.

At dawn the next morning, December 26th, Washington and his forces struck. Rall was indeed surprised. The British and their Hessian auxiliaries were unable to mount a proper defense. In the ensuing carnage, twenty-two Hessians lost their lives, while some eighty were terribly injured. Rall would receive a grievous injury and perish from his wounds. After the Hessians were defeated, almost one thousand prisoners of war were taken, along with a huge cache of weapons and ammunition.

After the successful execution of this daring attack, Washington had to lead the Americans and their booty back across the Delaware and into Pennsylvania. This daring victory was just what the Patriots needed and had a tremendous effect on morale. Prior to the crossing, some wondered if the war was lost, but afterward, it seemed that victory was all but ensured. The Battle of Trenton was small and didn't contribute much to the overall war effort, but it played a major role when it came to the psyche of the soldiers.

Nevertheless, the British rallied, and under Sir William Howe, the British forces were able to march on a revolutionary city of brotherly love, Philadelphia, in the summer of 1777. However, the British victory proved fleeting. The British forces in Philadelphia were ultimately defeated at the Battle of Saratoga that October. This victory convinced the French to side with the Americans. The French had been enemies of the British for a long time and were still smarting from their defeat in the Seven Years' War. They wanted to get their revenge against the British.

In many ways, it is ironic that the French king, who was himself an absolute ruler, would position himself to support a group of revolutionaries intent on thwarting the British king to whom they had been subservient. The French king could have cared less about the principles of the American Revolution. He just wanted to strike out against the British.

The full irony of his actions would be on display a few years later when France was rocked by the French Revolution, which had been inspired in many ways by the American Revolution. In the tumult of the French Revolution, the French king, who had supported the American revolutionaries, would ultimately be deposed and have his head cut off by the guillotine. But in the rush to punish the British, the finer details of what it might mean to support a revolution hellbent on overthrowing a monarchy did not seem apparent or matter to the French monarch.

The French contribution to the American war effort proved to be the decisive difference. Their aid cannot be underestimated. A joint French/American force gave the British their death blow at the Battle of Yorktown. In the fall of 1781, this combined force entirely encircled the British positions at Yorktown, forcing them to surrender that October.

During the assault, French naval forces waited at Chesapeake Bay while Washington and his soldiers cornered British General Cornwallis's forces on land. The British had nowhere to go and ultimately had to surrender. This was the last major battle of the war, and the full recognition of American independence by the British would occur soon after. This feat was realized with yet another Treaty of Paris. This time around, the 1783 Treaty of Paris affirmed the independence of the United States of America.

The war was over, but many of the military veterans who had fought and struggled so hard for the independence of the nation found themselves without pay and, more often than not, with nowhere to go. Upon the chaotic demobilization of the American militias, many were far from home yet left to figure out what to do with themselves. Many of these veterans who had no pay, food, or shelter showed up at what was the epicenter of the pre-revolutionary days:

Boston, Massachusetts.

The treatment of veterans back then and the treatment of veterans now are entirely different. Back then, to many who did not have to fight and remained safely ensconced in their communities, the veterans were often seen as nothing more than an eyesore. Citizens had kept a safe distance from the conflict and did not want these dirty, homeless veterans to remind them of the war now that it was over. There were no veteran programs in those days and no outreach.

Rather than being revered as today's veterans are, the revolutionary veterans were almost despised. Today, veterans are regularly lauded as heroes, and everyone is more than ready to show their support. But back in Boston, when homeless Revolutionary War veterans clogged the streets, they were viewed as more of a nuisance than anything else.

Since no one heard their pleas for help, many of these veterans took matters into their own hands. A veteran by the name of Daniel Shays was once thought to have rallied other veterans together in protest, culminating in the infamous episode known as Shays' Rebellion. Scholars have recently come to the conclusion that Shays' role in this rebellion probably was not as large. Nevertheless, the rebellion brought to light issues that the US government had been putting off, namely dealing with the Articles of Confederation.

To truly understand how things were back then, one has to realize the state of the country. The United States was a fledgling nation that had just barely thrown off British rule. Its institutions were in their infancy and did not yet have the capacity to effectively care for its veterans. There were no massive government programs to see to their needs, and many veterans, despite their service, had to do without. Those were simply the harsh realities of the times.

Another harsh reality was the fact that there were many pragmatic realists on both sides of the Atlantic that saw France, not Britain, as the greatest external threat to the region. Yes, it is ironic that the United States would ally with France only to view French ambitions with deep suspicion. Upon Britain's defeat, the Americans and the British seemed to realize that it was advantageous to them both to be on somewhat close terms with each other to prevent the French from attempting to make further inroads in North America. The Seven Years' War had finally pushed the French out (at least for the most part), and neither the British nor the Americans wished to see French domination return.

The Americans would fight the so-called "Quasi-War," during which unofficial military action was taken against the French from 1798 to 1800. By this time, the French Revolution had already erupted, and the increasingly concerned Americans found themselves having to fend off aggressive French actions in the Caribbean.

The French king had been executed in 1793, and the United States refused to support the country in its war against Britain, issuing the Proclamation of Neutrality that very year. In the minds of American officials, this rendered their many previous agreements with France that had been made during the American Revolution null and void. This included a pledge to keep the British out of the French Indies in the Caribbean, as well as any obligation to pay back French loans that had been doled out during the war.

Even though war was never officially declared, the US faced open hostilities with the French in the waters of the Caribbean. Initially, the French were quite successful in harrying and seizing American shipping.

However, the Americans were determined to get rid of the French menace and used its naval fleet, which had been first established in 1775, to specifically meet this challenge. The navy had limited objectives and was mainly used to police the waters and curb the aggression of the French. The actions of the Quasi-War are said to have set a precedent for future "police actions" and "undeclared wars" of the future.

Napoleon Bonaparte, who took over France in 1799, ultimately ended the squabbling between the American and French navies with the Convention of 1800, in which American neutrality was officially recognized and honored. America would sit out the rest of the subsequent Napoleonic Wars, content to let the British and French duke it out.

PART TWO: FROM REVOLUTION TO CIVIL WAR (1783–1865)

Chapter 3: The Early National Period (1783–1812) and the War of 1812

"The soldier is the army. No army is better than its soldiers. The soldier is also a citizen. In fact, the highest obligation and privilege of citizenship is that of bearing arms for one's country."

-George S. Patton

The factors that led to the outbreak of the second act of fighting with the British, the War of 1812, were largely due to simmering arguments over British territorial ambitions in what remained of their American colonies and British aid to Native American tribes and confederations, which had been actively thwarting the westward expansion of the American states. At this point, America was a fairly minor military power.

The Quasi-War against the French had forced the Americans to cobble together a defensive navy, but America was still not able to project its military might beyond its immediate borders. Even so, the Americans did conduct a limited military operation abroad in the year 1801 when they launched a punitive expedition against Barbary pirates who had been attacking American shipping in the Mediterranean.

The sultan of Tripoli had apparently come under the impression that the Americans were the weakest of the naval powers, and their ships participated in trade in his backyard. Like any bully, he decided to test his luck against those whom he perceived to be the most vulnerable. After several instances of American sailors being attacked, robbed, and kidnapped, the US decided that it was time to take action.

A small naval fleet was sent to the shores of Tripoli and proceeded to bombard the sultan's port to smithereens. The sultan finally had enough and sued for peace. This adventure on the shores of Tripoli would go on to inspire the lyrics to the "Marines' Hymn," which declares, "From the halls of Montezuma to the shores of Tripoli...."

Despite the Americans' success at showing the Barbary pirates who was boss, American shipping continued to face problems. The British continued to impress American sailors into service for the British military. For many Americans, this was an outrage that simply could not be tolerated.

The most infamous instance of British aggression in this regard occurred during the *Chesapeake-Leopard* affair. In 1807, an American ship called the *Chesapeake* was boarded by the British off the shores of Virginia. The British, who were still battling the French in the Napoleonic Wars, had apparently suspected the ship of smuggling supplies to the French.

The Americans were quite incensed by the act and denied the British access. The British were undeterred and simply commandeered the ship by force. This led to an outright gunbattle in which four Americans were killed. Adding insult to injury, after the arbitrary search, several of the sailors were forcibly impressed into service for the British.

But other than declaring war on Britain, there did not seem to be too much the Americans could do about it. Congress began moving steadily toward a declaration, and on June 18th, 1812, war was declared. The British took immediate action and imposed a naval blockade on America's ports.

The Americans attempted to strike back at the British on land by launching raids into British holdings in Upper Canada, but these were largely ineffective. The British assembled some six thousand crack troops to defend the region, and the militias that had been cobbled together by the Americans proved to be no match for them. The US did have a standing army by this point (it was created in 1789), but the government greatly relied on local militias to help boost their numbers.

Even worse for the Americans was when British General Isaac Brock hooked up with some Native American allies, who were led by a fierce Shawnee chief named Tecumseh. Tecumseh and his coalition were certainly a force to be reckoned with. Tecumseh was not only a great military strategist, but he was also a savvy politician and was able to unite Native American tribes in a manner that few tribal chiefs before him could.

Tecumseh was even able to bring together tribes that were normally hostile to each other. He believed the Native Americans needed to have a united front to face the threat of America's westward expansion—an expansion that would affect all tribes, regardless of their differences.

This allied group launched an offensive against Fort Detroit, and through simply instilling great fear in the defenders, they were able to seize the fortress without so much as firing a shot. As part of their ingenious strategy, Brock and Tecumseh arranged for a contingent of fierce Native American warriors to march all around the fort. The march was orchestrated to make the band of warriors appear more numerous than they were. They doubled back a few times to create the illusion of a vast multitude.

After this display, Brock sent a message to the man in charge of Fort Detroit, General William Hull, saying that he would try to restrain the "numerous body of Indians" from inflicting atrocities. However, he insisted that unless the fortress surrendered, he could not make any promises. Brock's crafty words stuck a chord with the fearful defenders of Detroit, and they decided to surrender.

Brock and Tecumseh gained over two thousand prisoners of war and were able to seize a large stockpile of weapons and ammunition. The Americans were enraged to learn of these humiliating developments. Perhaps wishing to recreate Washington's famous crossing of the Delaware River, a plan was hatched for American forces to cross the Niagara River and launch an expedition into Canada's Queenston Heights.

The Canadians were hard-pressed in this exchange, and Brock was killed. The British and Canadian forces were able to regroup and ultimately repulsed the American troops. This battle resulted in around one hundred Americans losing their lives, and almost a thousand men became prisoners of war. All in all, the beginning of the War of 1812 was a series of defeats and unsettling setbacks for the American forces.

The Americans were only successful in Northwest Territory, with sudden wins against the British in positions around Lake Erie and the Thames River. On Lake Erie, American Admiral Oliver Hazard Perry managed to deal a knockout blow to the British navy, disrupting the vital waterway that had long served British interests in the region. During the Battle of the Thames in 1813, Britain's ally, the Native American confederacy, received a mortal blow when Chief Tecumseh was killed. Although Native Americans still fought in the war with the British, they were more disorganized and did not fight as a united front anymore.

The British were still wrapping up their war with Napoleon, so they weren't able to fully dedicate themselves to the war in North America. After Napoleon was defeated in 1814, the full might of the British army began to descend upon the colonists. The British marched on Washington, DC, and set much of it on fire. The White House and the US Capitol were rendered into smoking rubble.

It has been said that the plans for the defense of the US capital had been severely neglected. In fact, it is believed that serious considerations were not even made until just a few weeks before the British attacked. On July 1st, 1814, the first plans were drafted, and a call for 100,000 militiamen was made to defend DC. Ultimately, only some eleven thousand answered the call.

This still gave the defenders a roughly two-to-one advantage against the British, but it was not enough in light of the well-disciplined and well-equipped British troops. The American militiamen who had shown up to defend DC at the last minute were a ragtag bunch and ill-prepared to fight. Orders were given, but they were not followed very well. Due to the American troops' sheer disorder, confusion, and, in some instances, cowardice, the British were able to tease a tremendous victory out of what should have otherwise been a sure defeat.

The destruction of the capital was not a knockout blow, and the nerve center of America was able to evacuate and move to higher ground. Strategically, the destruction of the capital was not as bad as what happened the following September when the British swooped down on Maine, seized part of it, and began using it as a forward base for further incursions.

American commanders were having trouble dealing with the less-than-enthusiastic soldiers under their command. Unlike their predecessors who fought in the freezing cold with threadbare clothes and little to no pay, those recruited for the War of 1812 were determined not to be pushed around by their commanding officers. During the War of 1812, many American troops learned the value of subtle insubordination.

There were instances in which large bodies of men would simply slow down their marches to such a leisurely pace that their commanding officers were ultimately forced to give in to various demands, such as better food and lodging. In more extreme situations, an actual mutiny was either implied or openly threatened until certain demands were met.

There was an incident on November 1st, 1812, when members of a militia led by Daniel Miller balked at the poor conditions of their camp. They picked up all of their equipment and began to openly desert. Miller, who was in charge of the outfit, ultimately broke down and caved to their demands. The soldier class and the officer class learned through trial and error to become a more mutually beneficial organization.

The next turning point in the war would occur during the Battle of Plattsburgh on Lake Champlain, where the British were soundly defeated. On the heels of this victory, the Treaty of Ghent was signed on December 24th, 1814, ending the war.

Even so, due to the nature of how slow word traveled back then, hostilities continued until the spring of 1815. After the war had officially ceased, at least on paper, General and future US President Andrew Jackson bested the British in the Battle of New Orleans.

At any rate, with the signing of the Treaty of Ghent, the British finally recognized the power of the United States and agreed to end the hostilities. In many ways, the British and the Americans were back where they had started, leading many to declare that the entire war was fairly pointless. However, one thing that the War of 1812 decisively determined was the evolution and trajectory of the US military. After the War of 1812, US officials began to realize just how outdated their militia system of fighting was.

It was clear that rather than having scattered militias that could not always be depended upon, a national standing army needed to be forged. A veteran of the War of 1812, Winfield Scott, who would later become a distinguished general in the Mexican-American War, literally wrote a book on how such things should be achieved. He wrote an entire training manual on the subject that would get much use in the years to come.

Chapter 4: The Texas Revolution and the Mexican-American War

"Discipline is the soul of an army. It makes small numbers formidable; procures success to the weak, and esteem to all."
-George Washington

Texas was once part of Mexico. It is a simple enough historically accurate statement, but it is surprising how many Americans are not aware of this fact. In the last few years that Texas and Mexico were joined at the hip, Mexico was going through many political changes and upheavals. Starting in the year 1833, Mexico was under the rule of a military general by the name of Antonio López de Santa Anna.

Santa Anna was just one of many struggling for power after Mexico cut the last of its ties to its former colonial overlord the Spanish Empire. The Spaniards had been given the boot, and a sizeable Mexican territory that stretched from its border with Central America all the way up into what is now considered the Southwest United States was up for grabs. All of Texas was part of this huge expanse.

Having said that, most of the Mexican frontier was sparsely populated and suffered from a lack of clear administrative control. The few who dared to live in the sparsely populated regions in the north, such as in Texas, did so at their own risk since raids from the local Apache and Comanche tribes were a common occurrence.

The situation was already so untenable that the Mexican government began to actively seek out American immigrants to populate the land. As this push to recruit Americans to tame the wild Mexican frontier regions went forward, some sixty-eight thousand Americans had settled in Texas by 1835. These were roughhewn souls who were used to depending on their own guns and wits for survival.

Unlike the folks in Mexico City, who were more reliant upon stores, police forces, and what little industry there was, these rough and rugged individuals in Texas sought to blaze a path for themselves entirely on their own. These self-sufficient frontiersmen were indeed quite good at settling the range—in fact, they were too good. It was not long into that fateful year of 1835 before the Texas Revolution broke out in earnest.

The main reason the Texas Revolution broke out was due to the Texan settlers' independence. As mentioned, they were self-sufficient and used to playing by their own rules. And it only took a little bit of pushback from the Mexican government for them to try and strike out on their own.

For example, in 1835, Mexican President Santa Anna repealed the previous Mexican Constitution and attempted to institute reforms that would have invested more power in the central Mexican government while dismantling local legislatures and thereby diminishing the say-so of Texans. The settlers of Texas were used to having their voice heard, so they were not going to stand for this.

The first real spate of fighting occurred in and around the town of Gonzales, Mexico, on October 2nd, 1835. The fighting erupted over Mexican troops wishing to repatriate a cannon that was in the possession of the Texans. The cannon had been temporarily given to the Texans to aid them in fending off Comanche raids in 1831.

However, the Mexican authorities grew weary of the Texans having this sort of firepower, and troops suddenly showed up to take it back. The Americans did not want this to happen and began to unload on the Mexicans. Two Mexicans were killed in this melee, and a general withdrawal was ordered.

This was only a lull in the fighting, as the Mexican Army prepared to go on the offensive. In the meantime, the leading lights of the Texan Revolution got together and began to draft their own constitution and forge a provisional government in November 1835. Texas was just a short walk away from declaring itself an independent republic.

In February 1836, Santa Anna, who was no longer president by this point, marched a large force army up to a place called the Alamo. Here, several Texans (around two hundred of them) were in place, just waiting for the Mexicans to arrive. This group was outnumbered, and it would only be a matter of time before they were whittled down. Nevertheless, they fought hard, and the Mexicans took some fairly severe hits.

General Santa Anna had some big plans. He figured that if the Alamo was smashed, it would be a short march to San Antonio. However, for that to happen, those holed up in the Alamo had to be killed to the man since they showed no willingness to surrender. Only fourteen people survived. One of the defenders, a man by the name of Robert Evans, was supposedly shot and killed when he was making his way toward a large amount of gunpowder with a flaming torch in his hand. It seems that Evans intended to blow the whole place up and take as many Mexican troops with him in the process. A bullet fired by Mexican troops ensured that he would not be able to do any such thing.

This heavy-handed takedown of the Alamo did not discourage the Texans; instead, it encouraged them. The Alamo became a rallying cry, with the Texans shouting, "Remember the Alamo!" as they prepared to carry on the fight. While the fight for the Alamo was still raging, on March 2nd, the Republic of Texas was officially declared to be independent.

Upon being made an independent state, a provisional interim president was selected, a man named David Burnet. Sam Houston became the chief commander of the Texas troops and would later become the president of the Republic of Texas. Houston realized he had a limited army at his disposal and sought to make the most of it. This meant he would not be able to march on Mexican positions directly, as he would risk sudden defeat. He knew he had to pick and choose his battles, utilizing hit-and-run-styled tactics.

Instead of heading toward Santa Anna, he moved away from him, heading off to the east. Houston was cornered at the San Jacinto River and was finally forced to face off against Santa Anna. It was at this point that Houston turned his full fury upon Santa Anna's troops. Although Santa Anna outnumbered Houston's troops three to one, the Texans fought so ferociously that they managed to decimate the Mexican military.

In a very short period of time, the tide turned. The Mexicans were routed, and the greater part of their army was destroyed. Even more importantly, Santa Anna was captured. While under duress and the threat of outright execution, Santa Anna was forced to recognize the independence of Texas. Although the Texans and later the Americans would use this to justify the seizure of Texas, Santa Anna understandably protested that he would not have done any such thing had he not (literally) had a gun to his head.

At any rate, Texan independence was declared and confirmed. The Treaty of Velasco, which Santa Anna signed on May 14th, 1836, determined that Mexican troops would head back over the Rio Grande, and everything north of the Rio Grande would be considered the territory of the Republic of Texas. Sam Houston was then elected the president of Texas on September 5th, 1836.

But the situation was essentially a stalemate, with Mexico ultimately not recognizing Texas and Texas refusing to give up its struggle for independence. The conflict was then reignited on March 5th, 1842, when around five hundred Mexican soldiers were sent into Texas and headed toward San Antonio. The situation would take on even greater gravity when the United States agreed to annex Texas into the Union.

Texas was officially admitted in December 1845. Mexico did not recognize this declared annexation any more than they had recognized Texas' original declaration of independence. Still, the tense standoff would continue for a few more months.

It was not until March of 1846 when President James K. Polk decided to test the limits of Mexico's patience by ordering US General Zachary Taylor to cross the Nueces River. This was a heavily disputed borderland at the time, and the presence of US troops there made war all but inevitable. The Mexicans viewed this as an outright invasion of their territory and struck back.

This was the start of the Mexican-American War. At the outset, the war did not go well for the Mexicans. Even though their armies were larger, the US troops had better artillery and were well trained. This would prove decisive during one of the first major battles of the war.

On May 8th, at the Battle of Palo Alto in the vicinity of the Rio Grande River, Taylor was able to run roughshod on his Mexican opponents by mowing down a large bulk of their troops with his highly efficient artillery.

The same thing happened the next day at the Battle of Resaca de la Palmoa, opening the door to the seizure of nearby Matamoros. The taking of nearby Monterey would be much harder, but after a few days of terrible, bloody fighting, it fell to the Americans as well. Very soon, the Americans had large swathes of what were the northern provinces of Mexico in their hands.

It was hoped that these dramatic gains would push the Mexicans to the peace table. But this was not the case. When it was clear the fight would continue, President Polk authorized General Winfield Scott to orchestrate an invasion of the Mexican capital, Mexico City.

Due to the tumultuous politics of Mexico, Santa Anna had since been exiled and then reinstated. Ironically enough, he was actually reinstated with the help of the United States! At the start of the war, Santa Anna had been living as a political exile in Cuba. But after he promised US President Polk that he would do everything within his power to negotiate a peace deal if he came back to Mexico, the navy opened up its blockade and allowed Santa Anna to land on Mexican shores.

As soon as Santa Anna reached the Mexican capital, he positioned himself as Mexico's ultimate defender and promised the Mexican people that he would lead the charge to drive the Americans out. Santa Anna became both the leading general and the leading statesman of Mexico as it struggled to shake off the Americans. In 1847, Santa Anna led the Mexican Army's offensive in Buena Vista.

He had forged a formidable army, said to be about fifteen thousand strong. The US force he was heading to intercept was only made up of some five thousand troops. Upon his approach, Santa Anna actually sent a message to General Zachary Taylor, demanding an immediate surrender to prevent further loss of blood.

You have to hand it to Santa Anna for at least trying to negotiate, but the Americans were not interested. General Taylor is said to have fired off a response in which he declared, "If you want us, come and take us!" The Americans fought ferociously, and through the strategic use of specially positioned artillery, they were able to drive Santa

Anna's forces off, but not without the loss of some 750 American soldiers in the process.

Zachary Taylor's stand at Buena Vista was considered bold but costly. Furthermore, it was largely unnecessary. Winfield Scott would put some of his West Point training to good use by executing a brilliant amphibious landing at the port of Veracruz. The landing was successfully achieved on March 7th, 1847.

In stark contrast to the American military's previous reputation of being ragtag and disorderly, the successful landing of a large contingent of troops under Winfield Scott demonstrated a high level of professionalism and efficiency, with troops and naval craft being perfectly orchestrated to make sure the amphibious landing went off without a hitch.

After this amphibious landing, a bolstered army of around fifteen thousand, with General Winfield Scott at the head of it, went down to the Mexican base of Chapultepec Castle. The fort was overrun, and from here, the Americans marched to Mexico City itself. Scott's troops achieved victory in Mexico City on September 13th, 1847. They occupied the capital, and the Mexican government soon capitulated. This defeat was official on February 2nd, 1848, with the signing of the Treaty of Guadalupe Hidalgo.

This time around, Mexico's defeat was complete, and there would be no claims of signing under duress; this was an official military defeat with official consequences. The treaty had Mexico cough up not just Texas but also huge tracts of land that would eventually become New Mexico, Arizona, and California, at least as we know them today. The United States did not want to be roving conquerors and offered some compensation for the territories, paying the Mexican government some fifteen million dollars in exchange. The war was over, and history had been made.

Chapter 5: The American Civil War

"Brave men rejoice in adversity. Just as brave soldiers triumph in war."

-*Lucius Annaeus Seneca*

In many ways, the Civil War had its roots in the largest conflict that preceded it, the Mexican-American War. The reason is due to the early American concepts of statehood. The ugly issue of slavery was also at the heart of the matter. In the first half of the 19th century, whenever a state was admitted to the Union, there was always a question over whether it would enter as a slave state or a free state (a state in which the practice of slavery was banned).

Texas was a slave state. It was largely for this reason that it took well over a decade for the Union to consider annexing Texas. There were those who wished for the annexation, both among Texans and in the Union, ever since the Texan Revolution kicked off in 1833. However, statehood was denied to Texas for several years out of fear that admitting another slave state would upset the balance of slave and free states.

The Mexican-American War granted the US huge new tracts of land, so the matter of which states would be admitted as free states and which as slave states was front and center. These tensions would continue to grow until the 1860 election, in which a Republican by the name of Abraham Lincoln was elected. The Southerners feared Lincoln because of his stance against slavery.

To be clear, Lincoln never stated that he would get rid of slavery, but he certainly intimated that he would try to limit it. He was in favor of ending the expansion of the practice into the western territories. However, the Southerners feared that Lincoln would bring the institution to an end. And shortly after Lincoln was elected, some Southern states seceded. This move would eventually lead Lincoln to initiate a call to arms, and the Civil War would begin. This American conflict would become both terrible and legendary.

For those who were actually on the battlefields and subjected to one of history's first mechanized military meat grinders, the war was far from glorious; it was downright frightening. The Civil War stands out as the first instance in which US troops faced slaughter on a truly industrialized scale. In previous conflicts, American troops saw perhaps a dozen or so comrades perish at a time.

But during the Civil War, hundreds could be easily mowed down in just one terrible skirmish. Civil War soldiers saw their peers ripped to shreds and trampled upon. Terrible moans filled the air as arms and legs were lost, and the stench of death filled their noses. Most of the troops were not prepared for what awaited them on the bloody grounds of this fratricidal conflict.

Many of these new recruits, who had been nursed on the patriotic stories of the American Revolution, were not expecting the nightmare that awaited them. Headlong heroic charges were exchanged for hunkering down in trenches. All-or-nothing battles were replaced with strategies that consisted of slowly chipping away at entrenched enemy positions.

It is worth noting the similarities and differences between the Union and Confederate armies. First of all, many of the officers on both sides of the conflict had been trained at West Point. Many of them had also fought together in the Mexican-American War. Union General Ulysses S. Grant and Confederate General Robert E. Lee both fondly reminisced about their service in this previous conflict during Lee's surrender.

The main difference was in the quality of equipment. The North was more of an industrial powerhouse than the South. The Union Army was well equipped and could easily produce arms and ammunition on demand, whereas the Confederacy often struggled to maintain proper equipment and even basic supplies. However, the Confederates were very passionate about what they were fighting for, as they believed their livelihoods were on the line. The Union wanted to win, of course, but not everyone fervently believed in the war, especially at the beginning.

Nevertheless, when the war began, both sides expected a quick and easy victory. Southerners who were itching for a fight infamously assaulted the Union-held Fort Sumter in April 1861. Those doing the assault were under the impression that the federal government of the United States would capitulate to their demands.

However, the newly inaugurated president, Abraham Lincoln, proved just how stiff his resolve was and began the mobilization for war. The two forces collided that July during the First Battle of Bull Run.

The confrontation was actually instigated by the Northerners, who were seeking a knockout blow against the Confederates. They hoped to cross into Virginia and march on the Confederate capital of Richmond. Blocking their path was a Confederate force camped at Manassas Junction led by Confederate General P. G. T. Beauregard.

The Northerners were so confident in the might of their army that families sat and had picnics so they could watch the fighting in the distance. Such things sound ridiculous to us today, and to be sure, it was fairly ridiculous back then. Even if the Northerners had won the battle, what would have prevented a picnic goer from having their ham sandwich blown out of their hands by accidental friendly fire?

Initially, the Union troops seemed to have the advantage. But the Southerners held on just long enough for reinforcements, led by Confederate stalwart Joseph E. Johnston, to arrive on the scene. A militia from Virginia led by General Thomas J. Jackson held strong. It held so strong that Jackson would earn the nickname "Stonewall."

In the face of this stronger-than-expected defense and the arrival of Johnston's Shenandoah reinforcements, the Northern army was ultimately forced to retreat. The retreat was not at all orderly, and the new Northern recruits became frantic as they fled the field. It seems that things became particularly chaotic when artillery fire toppled a retreating Union wagon.

All of this chaos opened the door for a vicious counterattack, so Union soldiers practically fled back to Washington, DC. And yes, all of those picnic goers had to run for their lives as well since the whole area was overrun by Confederate troops. The Southern newspapers would later make fun of the whole thing, referring to it as "The Great Skedaddle."

It was certainly no picnic. The First Battle of Bull Run indicated this war was going to be a bloody and violent one with no clear end in sight. It took the Union some time to regroup, but in the next round of fighting, Lincoln had the Union Army trying to make up for lost ground.

A series of offensives followed, such as the Battle of Hatteras Inlet Batteries, which took place that August. The Battle of Hatteras Inlet Batteries was of extreme strategic importance. The Union planned to utilize its navy to seize Confederate forts nestled in the North Carolina Sounds off the coast of North Carolina. The fortresses were bombarded and subdued, thanks in large part to the fact that the ill-equipped defenders ran out of ammunition.

The Union had gained an important foothold, which allowed the North to implement a naval blockade on the region and prevent Southern ships from having a base with which to conduct raids on the North. The seizure of this strategic piece of real estate served as a major morale booster for the North after the disastrous engagement at Bull Run.

In the spring of 1862, Union troops were eager to score another victory and once again went on the offensive. And in one of the next main exchanges to erupt, the Battle of Shiloh, the tenacity of both sides would be tested. This battle would also be famous for the efforts of General Ulysses S. Grant.

Grant was a West Point graduate and had served in the Mexican-American War. He had a complicated history afterward and temporarily dropped out of military service. He was reinstated just in time to lead the charge at the Battle of Shiloh. The Battle of Shiloh erupted on April 6th, 1862, in the reaches of southern Tennessee.

On the day prior, some forty thousand Confederates had marched toward the Union lines. Everything was becoming increasingly up close and personal, and Confederates began to try their luck, using Union troops as target practice. It was clear that a battle was imminent, and as soon as the new day of April 6th dawned, Confederate General Albert Sidney Johnston unleashed his army to engage the Union positions outright.

The forces collided near a church called Shiloh. Hence, the battle itself was later dubbed the "Battle of Shiloh." The battle, although expected, was sudden and intense in its ferocity. General Grant was said to have been taken a bit off-guard. He had just sat down to have some coffee when his chief of staff, Joseph Webster, alerted him that the enemy was approaching.

Grant very quickly got over his surprise. He put down his coffee and headed off to lead the troops in battle. Grant was a livewire during the exchange, riding from one point of the conflict to another, making sure that his troops held the line. Grant was known to be quite skilled on horseback, and his horse-riding skills enabled him to quickly ride from one side of the fray to the other. This last-ditch stand would be dubbed "Grant's Last Line."

Ultimately, the Union troops would prevail but at a considerable loss of life on both sides. Confederate General Johnston was killed during the battle. Grant would be heavily criticized for his belligerent refusal to change tactics. He also faced accusations that would plague him for the rest of his life—he was accused of being drunk. It was already known that Grant had a bit of a drinking problem, and detractors in the press were quick to suggest that perhaps Grant had been hitting the sauce during the Battle of Shiloh as well.

At any rate, after Johnston was killed, the Confederates attempted to regroup under General Pierre Gustave Toutant Beauregard (better known as P. G. T. Beauregard). Beauregard was unable to pick up any momentum, and the Union troops were able to steadily push the Confederates back. However, these gains came at a great cost, and it is said that the Union Army lost thousands of troops in the Shiloh campaign.

A similar quasi-draw would be eked out when General George McClellan led an expedition into Virginia. This push was meant to carve a path for the Union troops to march on the Confederate capital of Richmond, with an early knockout blow once again in mind. McClellan's advance was thwarted at the Battle of Seven Pines, which took place on May 31st, 1862. It was a ferocious battle in which both sides suffered many casualties.

Perhaps the most interesting thing about the meat grinder that ensued was the participation of the Union's Army Balloon Corps. The balloon was believed to be of value as a tool of reconnaissance. A small crew could be placed inside the balloon and sent aloft to spy on enemy positions. Of course, balloons present some fairly obvious vulnerabilities; one stray bullet could bring a balloon down. But from a safe enough distance, balloons proved they could be of some use.

Just a couple of days before the battle erupted on May 31st, one of the balloon engineers was able to get a clear view of a Confederate troop buildup in front of the Fair Oaks Train Station. The balloon continued to send messages about troop positions via telegraph until the battle actually erupted.

It is interesting to note this early use of the balloon as a tool of wartime reconnaissance in consideration of the fact that balloons are still routinely used by militaries all over the world. In early 2023, China was caught sending a spy balloon over sensitive US nuclear installations in Montana.

Despite the Union's innovation of balloon reconnaissance, the Confederates were able to push back Union troops. But as reinforcements arrived, both sides began to suffer staggering casualties. Confederate General Joseph Johnston was badly wounded and taken from the field. Ultimately, both sides were forced to pull back, and the exchange became little more than a bloody draw. It was once again obvious that the Civil War would not be won easily.

The bloody Battle of Antietam, which occurred on September 17th, 1862, perfectly encapsulated this bloody stalemate. The battle kicked off after General George B. McClellan's army chased General Robert E. Lee into Maryland before backing the Confederates into a corner at Antietam Creek.

Soon, Union General Joseph Hooker was launching a ferocious attack on the left wing of Lee's troops. Very little progress was made, but in the late afternoon, Union General Ambrose Burnside managed to seize a stone bridge and made some advancements against the Confederate positions. The tide was slowly turning against the Confederate forces, and a major turning point would occur in the summer of 1863 during the Siege of Vicksburg.

Confederate forces had been holed up in Vicksburg, Mississippi. On May 22nd, 1863, Grant launched a major offensive against the

Confederate positions. The Confederates hunkered down, and the assault devolved into a siege. By July, Grant had received some intelligence information indicating that there were some inside Vicksburg who would like to surrender.

The surrender of Vicksburg was finally achieved on July 4th, 1863. This was not only a major victory but also a massive undertaking. With the capitulation of Vicksburg, Grant had to take on some thirty thousand Confederate prisoners of war. Vicksburg would essentially become a prison camp. The defeat of Vicksburg just so happened to coincide with the deflection of George Pickett's charge at the Battle of Gettysburg. Both of these defeats would spell the end for the Confederacy.

Pushed farther and farther into Southern enclaves and with ports blockaded by Union ships, the Southern resistance was finding that there was literally nowhere to run and nowhere to hide. As the Union closed in on all sides, the Confederate capital of Richmond was abandoned on April 2nd, 1865.

Confederate General Robert E. Lee tendered his surrender to Ulysses S. Grant in the aftermath of the Battle of Appomattox Court House on April 9th, 1865. The Civil War was over, but it would take a long time to rebuild the rifts that had nearly torn the fabric of the nation asunder. Making matters even worse, just a few days after the South surrendered, President Lincoln was killed by an assassin named John Wilkes Boothe, making any notion of real reconciliation all that much harder to realize.

PART THREE: FROM THE END OF THE CIVIL WAR TO WWI (1865–1918)

Chapter 6: The American Indian Wars (1865–1891)

"The true soldier fights not because he hates what is in front of him—but because he loves what is behind him."

-*G. K. Chesterton*

The American Indian Wars is the general name given to the conflicts the settlers and the US government had with the Native Americans. Although these conflicts began back in the 17th century, we are going to take a look at the battles that took place around the time of the Trail of Tears to the Battle of Wounded Knee (also known as the Wounded Knee Massacre).

These exchanges were complicated ones, to be sure, but one simply cannot gloss over the fact that the United States instituted a fairly clear-cut policy of pushing indigenous inhabitants farther and farther west as "Manifest Destiny," the idea that it was the Americans' God-given right to settle North America, took hold.

The American Indian Wars were devastatingly cruel, with what could be considered war crimes being committed by both parties of the conflict. In the past, when the history of the conflict between American settlers and Native Americans was told, there always seemed to be an emphasis on Native Americans ambushing, scalping, and viciously slaughtering settlers. In later years, the atrocities committed by Native Americans were toned down or even entirely tuned out to focus on the atrocities committed by the federal government and the US Armed Forces in the effort to expand westward. According to these biased accounts, one would think that Native American tribes were entirely peaceful and nonviolent. And yes, some tribes were more peaceful than others. But to insist that every tribe sought peace flies in the face of the reality of tribal warfare, which had been occurring in North America long before the Europeans ever arrived.

In truth, it would be wrong to overemphasize the violence of one side over the other. In reality, Native Americans and the US government engaged in a bitter, ferocious campaign against each other in which both sides committed routine atrocities.

Even so, toward the end of the American Indian Wars, it wasn't uncommon for the veterans of the US Armed Forces and Native American veterans to develop a grudging respect and appreciation for each other. This was certainly the case with Buffalo Bill, a former scout turned promoter. He employed Native American warriors who previously wouldn't have thought twice about killing him as entertainers in his extravagant Wild West shows.

Buffalo Bill's life and exploits perhaps best demonstrate the real-life complexities that were at play during this time and place in history. As much as past historians would like to paint one side as all bad and the other as all good, the complexity of humanity and human motives shines forth when one considers someone like Buffalo Bill.

As mentioned, Buffalo Bill famously staged popular Wild West shows in which he acted out fighting scenes with his former foes. But several years prior, he played a role in a terrible conflict that erupted between a tribal confederation of Lakota Sioux and the Northern Cheyenne, often referred to as the Great Sioux War of 1876.

The fighting had erupted due to the US government acting in bad faith on a previous treaty. The Black Hills region in South Dakota had been allotted to the tribes, but once some trespassing gold prospectors found gold in "them thar hills," all bets were off. In a classic government betrayal of the Native Americans, the federal government suddenly demanded that the tribes move so that the valuable lands of the Black Hills could be requisitioned by the government.

To be fair to the US government, as bad as it might seem that it went back on a previous treaty, government officials were trying to be pragmatic realists with the situation. They knew that if they just sat back and did nothing, prospectors would pour in regardless and illegally infringe upon tribal lands in their bid to get gold. This would have created all kinds of problems. In order to avoid this, US officials attempted to enter into negotiations with tribal leaders to resettle them in a different region.

But, of course, one can easily understand the frustration of the tribal leaders. They felt double-crossed and were sick and tired of being yanked around by the federal government. Leading the charge of this resistance was Chief Sitting Bull. Sitting Bull would instigate General George Armstrong Custer's famous "last stand."

In the Battle of the Little Bighorn, Sitting Bull was able to ambush Custer and decimate an entire company of troops. But incredibly enough, despite all of this bloodshed, the US. Armed Forces would eventually come to terms with Sitting Bull, and he would, for a time, live on a reservation with his people. In more peaceful times, he would be tapped by Buffalo Bill to perform with him at his popular Wild West shoes.

Buffalo Bill saw the irony in all of this and touted the exhibition as "Foes in '76—Friends in '85" in recognition that although Sitting Bull was the great nemesis of the American army in 1876, he was now ostensibly on friendly terms.

At any rate, in order to understand the American Indian Wars, one has to delve into the roots of the conflict. The roots have everything to do with westward expansion. Even before it was American policy to expand westward, the first brave souls to make an attempt were individual settlers who pushed through dangerous frontier countries. These intrepid explorers forged famous trails, such as the Santa Fe Trail and the Oregon Trail, which took them westward into unknown and potentially hostile lands.

But even so, relations were not always bad. There were many instances in which settlers and Native American tribes got along fairly well with each other. Peace was officially established on the Oregon Trail by way of the Treaty of Fort Laramie, which was signed in 1851 by several Plains tribes and the United States. However, gold in the region led to the Pike's Peak Gold Rush of 1858, which saw many more settlers arrive on the scene and led to the treaty being broken. This massive influx of people was disruptive to the fragile relations that had been established between settlers and neighboring tribes.

The eruption of the Civil War in 1861 would bring industries out west, as huge railways were built to help facilitate commerce and troop movement. Immediately after the war, these railroads were used to transport more people and materials westward. As the railroads expanded, army forts were established at crucial junctures to safeguard those passing through.

It was not long before these army outposts began to have skirmishes with local tribes. During the many uprisings, powerful Native American leaders, such as Red Cloud, Crazy Horse, Sitting Bull, and the Apache firebrand Geronimo, would rise up and keep the US Army quite busy. The Apache, in particular, were quite good at raiding and would launch several raids against settlers and even army outposts.

After the Civil War came to a close in 1865, the US Army made it a priority to bring the West under control once and for all. It was at this point that it became official policy to "assign" all Native Americans in the West to reservations. The US Army was tasked with asking Native American tribes to accept life on an allotted reservation; otherwise, they had to use coercive measures to force them into doing so.

All of this was done under the auspices of the Interior Department and the so-called "Indian Bureau," which tasked "Indian agents" with making sure these things were accomplished. The Indian agent was an interesting figure in the West and could be said to have been part politician, part soldier, and even part social worker. The Indian agent became the direct intermediary between Native American leaders and the army. If any dispute arose, the Indian agent would be sent as an official representative to arbitrate some sort of agreement.

After the Civil War, one of the biggest offensives against a western tribe occurred in 1868 against the Comanche. Major General Philip Sheridan, who was the commander of the Department of the Missouri, launched an operation against the local tribes of the region. These engagements would start and stop until 1875 and take place throughout Colorado, New Mexico, Kansas, and even parts of Texas.

These skirmishes were fast-moving and typically on horseback. The same sort of fighting was also occurring simultaneously with the Apache and US forces under General George Crook, who was in charge of the Department of Arizona. The Apache would prove themselves to be cooperative and entirely formidable all at the same time. The Apache would frequently enter into agreements and then break them when they realized that the agreements were not as good as they thought.

You can't really blame the Apache since they were dealing with a weak hand, and many of the Apache leaders were extremely shrewd political strategists who knew how to make the best of what little leverage they had to work with. Apache leaders like Cochise, Mangas Coloradas, Victorio, and especially the wild and ferocious Geronimo were quite adept at this kind of deal-making.

Geronimo, in particular, had a routine of cutting peace deals with the United States in which he promised not to raid American settlements, only to immediately head south of the border to conduct punitive raids on the Mexicans. The subsequent protests from Mexico led US officials to order Geronimo and his Apache band to cease and desist.

Geronimo understood the border between the US and Mexico quite well, and for many years, he and his warriors used it to their advantage. They would attack one side of the border and then simply slip over to the other side, realizing that neither the Mexican Army nor the United States Army was able to effectively pursue them across the border.

All of this would change in 1882 when the US and Mexico, both sick and tired of these cross-border raids, signed a landmark agreement that would allow the cross-border pursuit of the Apache under the limited scope of targeting and stopping suspected bandits.

Victorio perished at the hands of Mexican soldiers in 1880, leaving the resistance largely in the hands of Geronimo. Geronimo would finally surrender to Crook's army in May 1883. Geronimo once again forged a peace treaty and agreed to join the rest of his people on the reservation. A couple of years later, he broke the treaty, went off of the reservation, and led a band of some 150 Apache to run roughshod over settlements in Arizona.

It was only in January 1886 that Captain Emmet Crawford, along with his own group of some eighty Apache scouts, caught up with them. Although Geronimo was cornered, he managed a daring escape. Indicating just how chaotic the situation was, Crawford perished shortly thereafter when he was shot by Mexican troops.

The Mexican troops were in pursuit of Apache raiding parties, and they apparently saw the encampment full of Apache scouts and mistook Crawford's contingent for being one as well. It's said that Crawford was desperate to correct the misunderstanding. He actually stood up on a boulder and waved a white handkerchief in the air. Sadly enough, he only made himself into an irresistible target and was shot in the head.

So, it was up to his second in command, First Lieutenant M. P. Maus, to corner Geronimo. He did so and amazingly was able to talk Geronimo into surrendering. However, this was just another ruse to buy time, and Geronimo was able to make a break for it a few days later. It was not until September of 1886 that First Lieutenant Charles B. Gatewood managed to get Geronimo to surrender to Brigadier General Nelson Miles. Geronimo and his remaining followers were sent off to a reservation, where they lived the rest of their days.

Demonstrating a surprising leniency that stands at odds with much of the previous harsh treatment of Native American leaders, Geronimo was not condemned for his actions. Despite the fact that he broke treaty after treaty, raided settlements, and killed many, he was essentially let off the hook. Upon his agreeing to join the other Apache on the reservation, he was allowed to go in peace. He did not like living on the reservation, but he made the best of it.

Geronimo even became a celebrity of sorts, occasionally going to Wild West shows, where he even went as far as to sign autographs for his "fans."

The last major gasp of major Native American resistance to westward expansion occurred in 1890 in the aftermath of the "Ghost Dance Movement." This was a religious movement that had been taken up by some tribes out west. The movement called for Native Americans to unite and do the "ghost dance," which, according to a popular prophet, would bring about the end of westward expansion.

In the midst of all of this, Indian agents had descended upon Sitting Bull's reservation to investigate some of the happenings of the movement. A confrontation occurred that quickly spiraled out of control, resulting in the death of Sitting Bull. Sitting Bull was sleeping when he was forcefully awoken by Indian agents who wanted to take him out of the camp. Sitting Bull refused, and a crowd gathered to witness what was happening. Someone shot an Indian agent, who, in turn, shot Sitting Bull. This event was later recalled by a historian and anthropologist named James Mooney.

Two weeks after Sitting Bull's death, on December 29th, 1890, the Wounded Knee massacre occurred. It is sometimes referred to as a battle, but the casualties were much higher on the Native American side, and most sources agree that it was a massacre. The Lakota traveling to the Pine Ridge Reservation were suspected of planning an uprising since they had partaken in the ghost dance soon before. They had their weapons confiscated. However, one man refused to give his weapon up. His weapon was fired, and the US forces began shooting the Lakota, who had just had all of their weapons taken from them.

The American Indian Wars lasted until 1924, although the fighting greatly decreased after the Wounded Knee Massacre.

Chapter 7: The Spanish-American and the Philippine Wars (1898-1902)

"Word to the Nation: Guard zealously your right to serve in the Armed Forces, for without them, there will be no other rights to guard."

-John F. Kennedy

The Spanish-American War and the Philippine War occurred in a rather rapid succession, starting in the year 1898. But in order to understand how these things came about, one needs a little background on the Spanish Empire in the Americas. The Spaniards, by way of Christopher Columbus, were the first Europeans to lay claim to territory in the New World. Some of the first territories that Spain seized were in the Caribbean. Resource-rich islands, such as Cuba and Puerto Rico, became the property of Spain.

The Caribbean was the forward base for further Spanish expansion. Spanish conquistadors landed in Central America and Mexico and battled with the indigenous populations for dominance. The Spaniards infamously toppled powerful civilizations, such as the Aztecs in Mexico and the Inca in Peru. Eventually, the Spanish conquest would bring a huge realm under Spanish dominion that consisted of most of South America, all of Central America, and

Mexico (including large portions of the modern-day southwestern United States).

Spain's reach would ultimately go even further. Springboarding off the western shores of the Americas, Spanish fleets landed in a chain of Pacific islands that would be dubbed the Philippines in honor of the Spanish monarch, King Philip II.

All of these lands would be under Spanish control until the rise of the French dictator Napoleon Bonaparte. Napoleon would shake Spain's grip loose of much of its overseas possessions. During the Napoleonic Wars of the early 19th century, Spain itself was overrun and occupied by the French.

This state of affairs prompted large portions of the New World territories formerly under Spanish control to become autonomous. Even after the Spanish monarch was restored to the throne and after Napoleon was defeated, these developments would have a lasting effect. There was a cascade of revolutions in Latin America, with one region after another declaring independence.

By the late 19th century, Spain had lost control of many of its former imperial possessions, save for some of its holdings in the Caribbean, the Philippines, Guam, and some islands off the coast of North Africa. By the outbreak of the Spanish-American War in 1898, Spain had been reduced to a mere shadow of what it once was.

The United States, in the meantime, had long been interested in the islands of the Caribbean. The notion of buying Cuba from Spain had been floated around for some time. And by the 1890s, the United States had quite a bit of financial investment in the region due to the booming sugar business. Cuban revolutionaries had been struggling to gain independence from Spain for some time, and many of them had been turning to the United States for help.

In 1898, Willman McKinley was president and sought to avoid being sucked into the drama. All bets were off when the USS *Maine*, which was sitting in Havana Harbor to protect American interests in Cuba, was mysteriously blown to bits on February 15th, 1898. Although it was not entirely clear how this event occurred (it is likely there was something wrong with the ship), the Americans were infuriated, believing Spain to be behind the explosion. Soon, there was a clarion call of "Remember the Maine! To hell with Spain!" McKinley ultimately gave in to this popular desire for aggression and declared war on Spain.

The war was a rapid-fire affair. War was officially declared on April 25th, and shortly thereafter, Commodore George Dewey, who had a squadron in the Pacific, famously outflanked the Spanish by destroying their outdated armada in the Philippines. With the Philippines secure, a major land invasion of Cuba was launched, with the US Army soon seizing Guantanamo Bay (which is still under US control).

Along with having a superior navy, the US Armed Forces also had superior firepower. US soldiers were readily equipped with both Colt-Browning M1895 machine guns and the Gatling machine gun.

These guns were blazing during the famous charge of San Juan Hill in early July 1898, which had none other than future President Theodore Roosevelt in the melee, leading his so-called "Rough Riders" into battle.

Roosevelt proved to be not only a natural leader but also a great promoter. He frequently spoke to the press and kept them fully abreast of all of the latest happenings. Members of the press were quite friendly with Roosevelt and readily conveyed all of his exploits to the public. These events caught the imagination of the public, and Roosevelt was soon one of the most popular figures in the nation. All of this acclaim would ultimately lead to Roosevelt being picked as McKinley's running mate in the 1900 presidential election.

Both the Spanish and the Americans and Cubans fought fiercely, although more American soldiers would perish from malaria than the war itself. Roosevelt penned a note to the Associated Press explaining in detail the state of affairs. Roosevelt stated, "Hardly a man has yet died from it, but the whole command is so weakened and shattered as to be ripe for dying like rotten sheep, when a real yellow fever epidemic strikes us, as it is bound to do if we stay here at the height of the sickly season. Quarantine against malarial fever is much like quarantining against the toothache."

Roosevelt then went on to state "that as soon as the authorities at Washington fully appreciate the condition of the army, we shall be sent home. If we are kept here it will in all human possibility mean an appalling disaster, for the surgeons here estimate that over half the army, if kept here during the sickly season, will die." These were some pretty stark words from Roosevelt, and fearing bad press, the

War Department took action.

The main hostilities had ended by August 12th, and the troops began the process of moving out. Many were sent to a medical camp of sorts that had been established in faraway Montauk, New York. The troops loaded up on boats and sailed all the way to Montauk, where they would be treated. However, upon the arrival of the first wave of sick soldiers, the camp realized it was woefully unprepared. It has been said that there were only a limited number of beds available for the vast multitude of men who had made their way to the camp.

The situation actually became so bad at the overcrowded camp that some men, out of sheer desperation, went AWOL (absent without official leave) and ran off to New York City, where many perished. The desperation of seeking to leave the camp by all means possible can be seen in a letter written by a veteran who spent time at the camp, Charles Post. He describes a scene in which a medic arbitrarily advised him to get out of his regular gear and into some camp-issued pajamas.

The pajamas looked more like inmate clothing than anything else, and many soldiers refused to wear them, fearing that it would only mean a longer stay. Upon being instructed to put on his pajamas, Post was warned of this very thing by a fellow soldier. As Post recalled, "The broken-winged soldier and I agreed that I must not get into my pajamas. 'You can't get out of this camp if you're in pajamas—you can't run the guard. You've got to get out. There's plenty help outside. Get yourself out!'"

Post then went on to say, "I swallowed the quinine pills, but I threw out the blue mass, a sort of compound cathartic made from mercury, I believe, and a very popular remedy nearly a century ago. It was the last medical examination, I believe, and a very popular hospital, and the last medicine. I knew that if I could get out, I could get word to newspapermen somewhere. Whatever the hospital camp had been intended to be, it was not; it was in utter breakdown."

This sad letter then summed up the poor fate of these sick veterans. Post bitterly remarked about how certain corporations who had contracted to build the poorly equipped camp had still made a profit. He stated that "Every dollar of their profits was flecked with the blood of dead and dying men." As it stands, more perished under poor conditions like this than they actually did on San Juan Hill.

This severe lack of preparation on the part of military planners would be under intense scrutiny and perhaps even congressional investigation today. Back then, though, American military officials simply sought to sweep the whole thing under the rug as quickly as possible.

Back on the war front, Spanish resolve had rather quickly collapsed under the rapid American onslaught, and a peace treaty was reached on December 10th, 1898. This treaty gave the US the territories of Guam, Puerto Rico, and the Philippines. Cuba was allowed to become an independent nation. The residents of the Philippines would have appreciated the same gesture, but the Americans were more content to simply replace the Spanish as the overlords of the region.

An underground Filipino resistance had long been brewing, and it would soon strike out at the American occupiers, just as it had against the Spanish. This resistance, led by Emilio Aguinaldo, was initially aimed at the Spaniards and had erupted in 1896, two years prior to the start of the Spanish-American War. Aguinaldo ultimately agreed to a truce with the Spanish and was exiled to Hong Kong. As fate would have it, in Hong Kong, Aguinaldo would come into contact with Commodore Dewey, who had a huge fleet of naval craft parked in the region, ready to launch an attack on the Spaniards in the Philippines.

Emilio Aguinaldo would later claim that Dewey verbally promised that the US would back Philippine independence, although Dewey would deny that any such agreement was ever made. At any rate, Dewey arranged to have the former rebel leader ferried to the Philippines, where he began to build up a homegrown group of Filipino revolutionaries.

This group actually declared the independence of the Philippines in the middle of the Spanish-American War, although the claim was essentially ignored by both the Spanish and the Americans. A little over one year after the 1898 Spanish-American War started, the Americans fought a war against Filipino revolutionaries that would become known simply as the Philippine-American War.

Filipino leaders would later claim that the US military had promised them independence, although no official written documentation exists to corroborate the claim. From their point of view, they were betrayed by the American occupiers. Instead of liberating them, as was the case in Cuba, the US betrayed the Filipinos by seeking to take over the Philippines for itself instead.

On February 4th, 1899, the first official fighting between the two sides began with the outbreak of the Battle of Manila. During this exchange, a Filipino group of armed insurgents charged at American positions in the city. The Americans were caught off-guard and forced to retreat. In their haste to clear the field, the Americans lost control of their artillery pieces, which were seized by the Filipinos.

Despite this early success, the Filipinos proved entirely undisciplined and disorganized. The following evening, the commanding officers on the Filipino side simply went home while the American forces regrouped, leaving the insurgents essentially leaderless. The American troops then stormed back and decimated the Filipino positions. Apparently noting the disaster that was unfolding, Filipino leader Emilio Aguinaldo demanded a ceasefire.

The Americans realized that the Filipinos had a losing hand and pushed the offensive forward. The Filipino troops were pushed back, and local towns and villages were seized. The Filipino troops had hoped for a general uprising of the populace to harry and hound the Americans, but for the most part, it never materialized. Soon the Americans were in complete control of Manilla itself.

However, that control was only kept through ruthless vigilance, which included rounding up and torturing suspected subversives. The fact that members of the Filipino resistance movement were tortured was no secret, and even the governor (and future US president) of the Philippines, William Howard Taft, openly admitted to as much when hauled before a Senate committee for questioning.

Taft spoke of how US service members employed the so-called "water cure" to get the truth out of suspected revolutionaries in US custody. The "water cure" was just another term for waterboarding.

Nevertheless, the Filipino resistance would continue until they were ultimately defeated in 1902. The fact that the Filipinos were able to carry on their struggle like this indicates a few things about the nature of the fight. First off, they had more passion. They were fighting for their independence, while the Spanish in the Spanish-American War were primarily fighting to hang onto a colonial possession for the Spanish Crown. Secondly, the Filipinos knew their land well and were able to better execute guerrilla warfare tactics to hamper the efforts of the US Armed Forces.

US policy shifted toward plans for the eventual independence of the Philippines. However, it would take a brutal Japanese occupation during World War Two to shake the grip of the Americans enough to recognize the complete independence of the Philippines after the Japanese were driven out.

Chapter 8: The USA Joins WWI (1917–1918)

"War is a horrible thing, a grotesque comedy. And it is so useless. This war won't prove anything. All we do when we win is to substitute one sort of dictator for another. In the meantime, we have destroyed our best resources. Human life, the most precious thing in the world, has become the cheapest. After we've won this war by drowning the Hun in our own blood, in five years' time the sentimental fools at home will be taking up a collection for those same Huns that are killing us now and our fool politicians will be cooking up another good war."

-Elliot White Springs, World War One veteran

The United States was late to the game as it pertains to World War One. The war kicked off in 1914, but it would take until 1917 for US soldiers to head into the fray. Before we delve into US participation in the war, it would be beneficial to discuss what led to the war in the first place. The factors are somewhat complicated, but the catalyst is easy to identify, as this war was triggered by one isolated event. Archduke Franz Ferdinand was visiting Sarajevo on June 28th, 1914, when he was assassinated by a Serbian nationalist by the name of Gavrilo Princip. This event would lead the Austrians to take a draconian stance against the Serbs and make several tough demands on the Serbians that they would never be able to meet. And upon Serbia's refusal to meet these demands, the Austrians declared war. This then triggered a domino effect of war declarations. Russia declared war on Austria, Germany declared war on Russia, and France and Britain declared war on Germany.

The Ottoman Empire would throw its lot in with Austria and Germany, thereby completing the Central Powers, which would face off against the Allies. Slowly but surely, most of the world was mobilizing for war. The United States remained resistant for a few more years, with many insisting that the war in Europe had nothing to do with America and that the US Armed Forces should do everything they could to stay out of it altogether.

Woodrow Wilson managed to get reelected as the US president on November 7th, 1916. Wilson had campaigned on keeping the US out of the war, but in quiet conversations with his associates, Wilson almost knew that US entry into the conflict was inevitable. Despite the US stance of neutrality, by 1917, German U-boats were prowling the Atlantic and threatening US shipping along the eastern seaboard. Such a state of affairs was intolerable, and it would not be long before the Americans were pushed into the war.

Unrestricted submarine warfare by German U-boats began in earnest on February 1st, 1917. It was believed by the German high command that if all shipping to Britain was targeted, the British would soon be knocked out of the war. This, of course, meant that all ships, regardless of their nation of origin, would be in the crosshairs. Some argued that such actions would bring the United States into the war, but others insisted that even this blatant aggression would not be enough to mobilize the US Armed Forces.

But in the possibility that the US was drawn into the war, German officials tried to cook up a scheme to thwart the Americans on their own soil. German State Secretary for Foreign Affairs Alfred von Zimmermann fired off the infamous "Zimmermann telegram" to Mexico in January 1917. This telegram laid out a plan in which Germany would support a Mexican assault on the southwestern United States.

The Germans had apparently been reading up on history and were essentially offering to aid Mexico in regaining the territory it had lost in the Mexican-American War. If such a front could be opened, it would have been a welcome distraction for the Germans, who did not want to see Americans landing in Europe. However, the

Zimmermann telegram was intercepted by the British, and by mid-February, it was fully deciphered by British intelligence.

The contents alarmed the Americans. This startling development was used by the war hawks in DC to push for America's entry into the war. Even so, there were some who held out. Some even suggested that perhaps the British were somehow pulling a fast one on them and that the whole thing was a hoax.

Interestingly enough, even this refuge of denial was eviscerated when a couple of days after the British relayed the contents of the telegram, none other than Zimmermann declared that the content of the message was genuine. The Germans let the Zimmermann telegram stand as a blatant and unabashed affront against the United States of America. And while US officials still debated the merits of war, on February 25th, a German submarine decimated the ocean liner *Laconia*, resulting in the deaths of two American citizens.

With all of this in mind, the US Senate voted on whether or not to go to war on April 4th, 1917. The results were quite clear. Eighty-two senators voted for war; they were opposed by just six. A couple of days later, the House of Representatives had its turn, and the results were very similar. Over 370 congressional representatives voted for US entry into the war, with only 50 opposed.

That very day, April 6th, an official declaration of war was made. Even so, it would take some time to mobilize, and the first step was to find a commander for this fighting force. That task was ultimately given to General John J. Pershing. Ironically enough, considering the Zimmermann telegram, Pershing had just come off an unofficial military operation in Mexico. Pershing was at the head of the punitive expedition to find the renegade Pancho Villa. Pershing was now going to use his experience as a commander to lead US troops into the uncertainty of the Western Front in continental Europe.

Before even arriving in France, a couple of hundred American troops landed in Britain on May 18th. They were not combat troops but rather medics who would help staff a base hospital. On May 26th, 1917, the first US combat soldiers showed up in France, numbering just over a thousand. This was just the first wave of many to come. In fact, as Pershing made his way to the European theater of war by way of ocean liner on May 28th, he was already drawing up plans for an army of at least a million men.

A huge batch of troops arrived the following month on June 26th. Some fourteen thousand American soldiers made their way to the shores of France, landing at St. Nazaire. But although these were combat troops, it was a bridge too far to say that they were combat-ready. On the contrary, it would take considerable time to train, arm, and get these new recruits up to speed. General Pershing was well prepared for the task and immediately set up an extensive network of training facilities in which to drill these fresh-faced troops.

By August, Pershing had hammered out a basic gameplan of how American troops would do their part in the Western Front. On August 20th, the so-called "General Purchasing Board" was established, which was allocated to fund the acquisition of war materiel. Soon after its establishment, the board managed to procure some 5,000 aircraft and some 8,500 trucks, which were scheduled to be put into action in June 1918. The initial American operations were not planned to be executed until the spring of 1918.

Shortly after these combat maneuvers commenced, a German air raid was conducted against a British base hospital that housed Americans. Four Americans turned up dead.

Initially, before the Americans had their own troop formations ready, American troops were being actively tapped to join active British and French contingents. Although minor in scope and operation, this was perceived as a great boost to the Allies.

Interestingly enough, Britain faced a shortage of manpower and was actively attempting to recruit out of Ireland. Due to the already strained relationship between England and Ireland, there was considerable pushback against any such measure being taken. It was considered especially egregious that the Irish were being forced into service in light of the auxiliary boost of American troops on the ground.

Famed poet William B. Yeats remarked, "I read in the newspaper yesterday that over 300,000 Americans have landed in France in a month, and it seems to me a strangely wanton thing that England, for the sake of 50,000 Irish soldiers, is prepared to hollow another trench between the countries and fill it with blood."

On April 20th, 1918, a large group of American troops first saw considerable action. They were positioned around the French village of Seicheprey when they were suddenly beset by some 2,800 German soldiers. The American force only consisted of around 655 troops.

These soldiers were literally outnumbered four to one, and defeat was almost certain. The fact these troops were nearly obliterated in this exchange brought much criticism from both Pershing and his European counterparts. Despite the fact that the troops were overwhelmed by a larger contingent, Pershing felt that leadership and bravery had been lacking.

French and British officers were even more brutal in their critique and often tried to write off the Americans as unprofessional and incompetent. The Americans were held in such disdain that many British and French officers insisted that American help could not be depended upon. It is perhaps somewhat hard for us to imagine such things today, considering the fact that the US military has been essentially considered the number one fighting force on the planet since the end of the Second World War. But at the start of World War One, this was simply not the case.

The US Army was ranked seventeenth in the world, far below the likes of Britain, France, and Germany. And even though the US boasted a healthy population, the numbers that regularly filled the US Armed Forces was typically little more than 100,000. This fighting force was good enough for regional conflicts, such as the Spanish-American War in Cuba or even Pershing's own punitive expedition in Mexico. But at this point in time, America was essentially just a regional power and struggled to effectively project itself on the world stage.

The equipment of the US Armed Forces steadily evolved. Ironically, the American model 1903 Springfield rifle, which the Americans used during World War One, had been based on the highly effective German Mauser guns. Americans were exposed to these weapons during the Spanish-American War, as it was the weapon of choice for the Spaniards. As it pertained to modern machine guns, the US troops were largely handed French models, such as the notoriously untrustworthy Chauchat, which was known to jam at the most inopportune of times. Nevertheless, the Americans tried to make the best of it, even though conditions were not always ideal, and their European allies were not always forthcoming.

Because the European officers became increasingly disdainful of the American soldiers, a rift developed between Pershing and his

European peers. Pershing was ready to get the Americans up to speed to stand on their own as a strong fighting force, but his European counterparts were doubtful of American strategic leadership and wished to absorb American manpower under their own leadership. It was argued that if the Americans were left to their own machinations, precious ground might be lost.

However, Pershing was willing to stand up for his troops. When confronted about the risk of losing ground, he angrily declared, "Yes, I am willing to take the risk. Moreover, the time may come when the American army will have to stand the brunt of this war, and it is not wise to fritter away our resources in this manner."

It could be said that the "time" Pershing spoke of came in June 1918 when the American forces became locked in mortal combat with German troops located in the vicinity of Belleau Wood. The battle was a fierce one, and the outbreak of it was captured quite well by a soldier who experienced it, Private E. A. Wahl. Wahl wrote a letter home in which he essentially gave a play-by-play of how the Battle of Belleau Wood transpired.

Wahl stated, "Just as the day was breaking, about 3 AM of the 4th, we drew up in the main street of a little deserted village in the midst of the boom and flash of big guns. We climbed out with our machine guns and equipment and trailed off into a little near-by-woods. Excitement began to drive away our weariness then. We were told to rest, and that we wouldn't be going into the lines until evening. Managed to sleep for a couple of hours, but the roar from the artillery and machine guns in front became so heavy as the day advanced that rest was impossible. Stretchers with wounded French marines began coming up from the lines. Ambulance after ambulance dashed down and dashed back again. We realized that we were at last in the thick of things."

This is perhaps the best way to sum up that ever-so-striking realization that war is real. As Wahl tells it, "About noon a couple of high-explosive shells dropped near us. Then another and another. We were caught in an enemy artillery barrage that lasted about two hours. Our first casualty occurred then, a Corporal Johnson was hit by a piece of shell through the back, and died a few minutes afterward. We sought shelter everywhere, falling flat on our faces as we heard shells come screeching down. That was our only protection. We just had to lie flat wondering if the next was going to get us. One shell landed about fifteen feet from me and exploded. I heard a scream at the same time and looked up. It had landed in a hole where two chaps from another company were lying. Several of us rushed over to the spot and pulled them out. They were horribly cut up, but not dead ... I can't begin to describe my state of mind—you will just have to imagine it. We were getting our first real taste of the horrors of war."

Yes, nothing can really prepare one to see the true "horrors of war." To see men torn limb from limb, lying in a pool of their own blood—this is the stuff of nightmares and the cause of many cases of what today we might call PTSD. At the time, Private Wahl had no good way to describe the utter shock he felt upon living through this terrible experience. And it was an experience that every soldier, no matter what side he fought for, knew.

In his remarks, Private Wahl manages to express sympathy for his foes who were caught up in these terrible circumstances of war. Wahl ended his observations by stating, "The Germans have suffered terribly, though. Whenever we have made an advance and taken over positions evacuated by them we find their bodies lying about everywhere."

While this terrible battle was still shaping up, French General Ferdinand Foch began to demand that Pershing put five American divisions under French command. Pershing was adamant in his denial, insisting that the Americans would do much better with their own leadership. However, Pershing was not naïve and knew that in order for the Allies to be victorious, the American troop numbers on the ground would have to be increased.

But even while these plans were being made by Pershing, an invisible enemy was taking root. During the summer of 1918, a terrible outbreak of influenza erupted, which would lead to more troop deaths than any actual engagement on the battlefield. Despite the terrible sickness that was erupting on all sides, the Germans decided to go ahead with a major, last-ditch offensive. The German high command rolled the dice, and in 1918, they were ready to go for broke, hoping to somehow turn the tide of the war.

This major offensive was launched in March. By this point, the Germans were defying the norms of warfare by using poison gas against their opponents. They had first employed it in 1915 and would continue to do so throughout much of the war. And they were not the only ones. Research into mustard gas at American labs produced promising results that ended up having US battalions employing the chemical weapon on the field as early as 1918. The Spring Offensive saw the Germans gain some ground, although that would change during the Hundred Days Offensive, which began in August.

By the fall of 1918, the Central Powers had apparently seen the writing on the wall, and the leaders of these nations decided they better begin to look for a means to extract themselves from the conflict. They initially turned to the Americans in hopes of brokering some sort of last-minute peace. On October 3rd, 1918, a peace note was sent to US President Woodrow Wilson on behalf of Germany and Austria.

The note was a direct effort to send out feelers for what it would take to begin the process of a cessation of hostilities. The note wanted to, more or less, end the conflict without the Central Powers losing any of their territories or making any further concessions. Of course, this was not to be, and all involved on the side of the Central Powers would face severe consequences when an armistice was finally signed.

On November 11th, 1918, the fateful armistice to end the Great War was reached. The deal would immediately cause a cessation of fighting. It was famously enacted at the "eleventh hour of the eleventh month" of 1918. The terms of this armistice would later be finalized with the Treaty of Versailles, which was signed on June 28th, 1919.

Ultimately, the Central Powers would lose quite a bit. Both the Ottoman Empire and the Austro-Hungarian Empire ceased to exist. Germany would lose land holdings and have the Rhineland occupied by Allied forces. Since Germany was seen as the major instigator of the belligerence, it was also made to pay substantial reparations.

These reparations would strain an already stressed German economy, and in many ways, the harsh terms of the Treaty of Versailles would set the stage for World War Two. Due to the treaty and the Great Depression, which broke out in the late 1920s, extremism flourished in Germany.

American veterans had considerably mixed feelings about their wartime experience. Some felt they had somehow served the greater good—as vague as those sentiments might have been—but others could not help but feel as if they had been mere cannon fodder. They were nothing more than hapless bodies thrown into an entirely pointless meat grinder.

The United States government did take some measures to better care for veterans, with Congress allocating some nine million dollars toward the establishment of new rehab clinics and hospitals. There was also the establishment of the Veterans Administration to handle the massive influx of wounded veterans.

This was necessary since so many had been injured or fallen sick during their time overseas. However, this improved treatment of veterans would not last, and by the time the nation was in economic decline due to the Great Depression, veterans found themselves denied the financial rewards they had been promised.

Veterans had been promised bonuses and began to demand them during the economic difficulties of the Depression. These veterans were so serious about collecting their money, and in 1932, thousands of them went to DC to demand it. They were dubbed the Bonus Army.

This protest, which saw forty-three thousand demonstrators take part, alarmed many. Major George S. Patton was pulled to lead a cavalry charge against the demonstrators. It must have been a bitter slap in the face to these men who fought so bravely in the world war to be dispersed by the military. The veterans had to wait another four years before they were finally given their bonuses in 1936.

PART FOUR: FROM WWII TO THE WAR ON TERROR (1941-2019)

Chapter 9: WWII: Becoming a Superpower

"We must never forget why we have and why we need our military. Our armed forces exist solely to ensure our nation is safe, so that each and every one of us can sleep soundly at night, knowing we have 'guardians at the gate.'"

-Allen West

There are many factors that led to World War Two, and by and large, many of them can be said to have stemmed from the unfinished business of World War One. The losers of World War One were left bankrupt and bereft of much of their former territory. Ironically enough, even the winners would find themselves losing in the 1930s after the stock market crash that led to the Great Depression.

Even so, all the nations that would ultimately take part in World War Two managed to set aside considerable sums to build up their armed forces. In the United States, Franklin Delano Roosevelt (also simply known as FDR), who was elected in November 1932, promised to salvage the wreckage of the American economy. Under his guidance, the US Navy was rebuilt. FDR, like his distant cousin Theodore Roosevelt before him, had also served in the navy, acting as the assistant secretary of the US Navy.

Despite any campaign rhetoric to the contrary, FDR knew from personal experience just how important a robust navy was. And he quietly built up the US fleet all the way until the bombing of Pearl Harbor on December 7th, 1941.

Of course, World War Two didn't start with Pearl Harbor. It actually was rooted in conflicts that broke out in the early 1930s, with Japanese aggression in China, Italian aggression in Ethiopia, and German belligerence in the Rhineland and Sudetenland. But for most, the start of the war is considered to have been 1939, when Germany invaded Poland, leading Britain and France to declare war.

France would be subsequently knocked out of the war a year later, leaving Britain to face the Germans alone. Hitler would open a new front by invading Russia in the summer of 1941. However, it was not until that fateful day at Pearl Harbor on December 7th, 1941, that the United States decided to take on not only Japan, which was behind the attack, but also Germany and Italy.

The soldiers stationed at Pearl Harbor and other far-flung outposts in the Pacific realized they were suddenly at war with some of the world's most powerful militaries, and that realization must have been absolutely jarring. One soldier, Second Lieutenant Robert T. Smith, jotted his thoughts and feelings into his journal the very next day.

He had this to say, "Boy did all hell break loose today?! We all went over to the line after breakfast, and about 7 o'clock somebody ran in to the ready room and said the U.S. was now at war with Japan. We could hardly believe it even though it was confirmed on the radio. Everybody stood around laughing and kidding about it, although it was easy to see there was really plenty of tension. Here we are in the middle of the works now—with the Japs pounding Hawaii, Manila, Singapore and Thailand—60 miles away. Plans were made for our squadron to go to Rangoon, as they need more support for the R.A.F. [British Royal Air Force] there. If they don't bomb our field here before we get away, we'll be lucky."

Smith was located in China at the time of his remarks; he was working as a military advisor for the famed "Flying Tigers." The Flying Tigers were a group of US fighter pilots who were recruited to fend off the ongoing Japanese invasion of mainland China. Aid to China and anywhere else suffering from Japanese aggression would be done in the open.

This fact was alluded to in the lieutenant's memo when he mentioned that he and his group might be sent off to aid the British

RAF that were being pummeled by the Japanese in various British outposts in the Pacific. In many ways, the British and, to some extent, the French were the primary targets of Japanese aggression in the region. The Japanese wished to seize European colonial territories that were rich in minerals and other resources.

The attack on the United States at Pearl Harbor was largely a distraction and a bid to preemptively thwart a US response. With the US Pacific fleet crippled at Pearl Harbor, the Japanese felt they had a free hand to invade British, Dutch, and even French possessions in the Pacific. The Japanese also helped themselves to American-controlled Philippines. Japan had long been eyeing the Philippines, wishing to incorporate the islands into its empire. Now was its chance.

The attack on Pearl Harbor could have been a lot worse, especially if aircraft carriers had been present during the onslaught. But fortunately for the Americans, none of their aircraft carriers were at Pearl Harbor at the time due to adverse weather conditions.

The US military presence in the Philippines was isolated, and after Pearl Harbor, the Americans there did not have any hope for immediate reinforcements. So, it was with grim apprehension that those on the ground faced an all-out invasion by the Japanese on December 8th, 1941.

In the meantime, Germany and Italy honored their commitment to Japan by declaring war on the United States. Thus, the US was not just facing down the Japanese in the Pacific but was also heading off to the European theater.

But since there was no Western Front in France to land in since France was occupied by the Nazis, they had to take a detour to North Africa first. Unlike World War One, which had landing sites in France open and ready for the arriving Americans, this time around, US troops had to blaze their own path. They disembarked on North African shores on November 8th, 1942, nearly a full year after the Japanese assault on Pearl Harbor. They would land in what was formerly French territory, where they gained a foothold and then took on the Italians and Germans who had overrun North Africa.

The British had already been fending off the Axis advance from their outpost in Egypt, so it was planned for both sides to push back and meet up with each other. The US troops on the ground would become used to the old military motto of "hurry up and wait." Many who landed in North Africa found themselves spending several days at a time in camps, waiting to be given their next batch of marching orders. These periods of idleness would be interspersed with terrible fighting that could erupt seemingly out of nowhere.

Over in the Pacific, the Japanese were making inroads. They had taken over the Solomon Islands in the spring of 1942 and were even pushing toward nearby Australia. Protecting Australia was of great concern to the Allies, which included Australia. If Australia fell to the Japanese, the whole situation might become very bad for the Allied war effort.

The Japanese advance was ultimately stopped at the epic Battle of Midway, named as such because it took place near an island that was roughly midway between the United States and the Japanese home islands. It was a turning point in the war, and even though Japan had made significant gains up until this point, it would be dealt a devastating blow that would ultimately halt its advance.

Up until the Battle of Midway, Japan had seized much of coastal China, Hong Kong, British Malaya, the Philippines, Singapore, and even Indonesia (then called the Dutch East Indies). At the Battle of Midway, the Japanese were seeking to draw the vast bulk of US forces, in particular naval aircraft carriers, into the attack, hoping to sink as many as possible to prevent further US advances.

However, the US did not fall for this ruse and kept many of its best naval craft out of the conflict. They did this knowing full well what the Japanese attack plan was since Japanese coded messages had already been deciphered by US military intelligence. The Japanese were not aware that they had been found out, and ironically enough, their intended trap for the Americans turned into a trap for themselves.

Japan's most surprising and stunning maneuver during this episode was the landing of Japanese troops in the Aleutian Islands. This was meant to serve as a distraction at the very least and as a forward advance that could secure major parts of Alaska for the Japanese at best. If Japan gained a solid foothold in the islands, it could use the base to prevent US bombers from flying out of Alaska to bomb Japanese targets. It could also use the base to potentially bomb the United States.

The invasion of the Aleutian Islands was meant to coincide with the Battle of Midway, but the orchestration of the two events was poorly timed, resulting in a premature invasion of Alaska launched nearly a full day before the Battle of Midway even commenced.

The Japanese proved to be unready when a large contingent of US naval and airpower began to pummel them at Midway. Rather than blowing up US aircraft carriers, it was the Japanese aircraft carriers that sustained terrible damage. The Japanese aircraft carriers that were sunk that day included the ships: Akagi, Kaga, Hiryu, and Soryu. After this disaster, Japan would essentially be on the defensive for the rest of the war; meanwhile, the Americans inched closer and closer to the Japanese home islands.

In the meantime, the Allies had leapfrogged from North Africa to Sicily and on into the Italian Peninsula. They pressured Italy into surrendering on September 8th, 1943. This surrender was done in the name of the Italian king, Victor Emmanuel III, as well as a newly appointed prime minister and former general, Pietro Badoglio. The former prime minister, the fascist Benito Mussolini, had actually been ousted from power and placed under arrest. Mussolini would later be freed in a daring raid by German paratroopers. The Germans would then seize northern Italy and install Benito Mussolini as a puppet dictator. The US troops would secure their positions in southern Italy and make the slow trek north up the Italian boot.

The Allies were making plans to land in western Europe on the beaches of Normandy. This feat, known as D-Day, would be achieved on June 6th, 1944. The Germans had been preparing for this invasion for a long time and had established some rather formidable defenses. Machine gun nests were stretched all along the coasts, ensuring that American and other Allied service members would land in a buzzsaw of bullets.

Nevertheless, the US had made considerable preparations, and the Americans, with some 150,000 troops stationed on around 7,000 different naval craft, along with 15,000 aircraft flying overhead with paratroopers at the ready, landed in the thick of it.

Even in the face of seeing their comrades mercilessly mowed down by bullets, these brave men slogged through the coastal waters and onto the beaches, pushing through the pain and devastation until they managed to establish a beachhead. This tenacious foothold on the beaches of Normandy, France, would serve as forward bases and spell the beginning of the end for the German war machine. The last-gasp

German offensive to stave off this advance occurred on December 16th, 1944: the infamous Battle of the Bulge.

The Germans slammed into the American advance, hoping to create a "bulge" in their center that could be exploited. Interestingly, just before this major battle commenced, the Germans actually went as far as to drop a couple of hundred Germans behind enemy lines dressed up as American soldiers. They were apparently meant to somehow infiltrate the US Armed Forces. This strange effort is not talked about much, but some of the veterans of the war would later confirm the account.

According to one World War Two veteran, Lieutenant Arthur C. Neriani, the American troops developed a special kind of protocol to sniff out these would-be spies in their midst by asking pointed questions to the disguised Germans. A favorite was to ask, "What's a jelly bean?" Even if the German was knowledgeable enough to explain what a jellybean was, the German accent was typically unable to pronounce it since, in German, the "j" sound of English sounds more like a "y" sound.

So, instead of "jelly," the Germans would say something that sounded more like "yelly." And after the spies spoke of "yelly beans," they were taken into custody and denied their chance at finding information behind American lines.

At any rate, the Battle of the Bulge, as terrific as it was, did not manage to stall the American advance. Even after the Germans threw everything they had at the Americans, the American lines might have buckled a bit, but they held firm. The British Armed Forces, namely the 21st Army Group, and the US Third Army suddenly wheeled around and headed to the snow-covered Ardennes Forest in Belgium to relieve their American allies, who were sustaining the full brunt of the assault.

And soon, the Allies would close in on the Germans from both sides. American, British, and French forces approached from the west, and the Soviets came from the East, closing in on the German capital of Berlin in 1945. Hitler committed suicide in his bunker on April 30th of that year, and his successor, German Admiral Karl Dönitz, offered Germany's unconditional surrender a few days later.

Japan would struggle for a few more months. The Americans were heavily involved in the Pacific theater, engaging in major battles in Okinawa and Iwo Jima, to name a few. However, it was the threat of a joint American and Soviet invasion and the dropping of two nuclear bombs on the Japanese islands that convinced the Japanese to finally give up the fight. With Japan's formal surrender on September 2nd, 1945, World War Two was over.

Even so, two of the victorious Allies—the United States and the Soviet Union—would soon find themselves locked into a bitter dispute over the shape the post-world war order should take.

Chapter 10: Post-War Reformations

"The veterans of our military services have put their lives on the line to protect the freedoms that we enjoy. They have dedicated their lives to their country and deserve to be recognized for their commitment."
  -Judd Gregg

If anything could be said with absolute clarity about World War Two, the post-war outcome was much different for America than it had been in the previous world war, especially as it pertains to the strength of the US Armed Forces and the treatment of US veterans. Unlike the end of World War One, which saw US veterans shuffled off to the side and often denied the most basic of benefits, numerous programs emerged after World War Two. The sixteen million men and women who served in the war would have some kind of assistance when they returned home.

The Veterans Administration received massive funding, allowing for health care and education to be given to returning troops. The G.I. Bill, which allowed former service members to attend school with their tuition fully paid, was a breakthrough for many who otherwise never would have dreamed of going to college. The mood of the triumphant Americans was also much different since the outcome and, more importantly, the reason for the war in the first place were much less ambiguous than in past wars.

After World War One, many wondered what the war had even been about. To many Americans, it was sparked by the assassination of some little-known duke, which caused antiquated European alliances to spiral out of control. Of course, the reasons behind World War One were more complex than that, but Europe was an ocean away. The events that unfolded there did not impact the United States in the same way as it, for instance, Germany or France.

However, World War Two was different. After the horrors of the Holocaust were truly revealed, the justification for the Allies going to war against the Axis became much clearer. Those who fought in World War Two had no confusion about their role; for them, it seemed they were in a fight against evil. And considering the atrocities committed by the Germans, Italians, and Japanese, it is hard to argue that point.

Veterans also greatly benefited from the comprehensive Depression-era programs of US President Franklin Delano Roosevelt. Although Roosevelt would perish in office from a stroke on April 12th, 1945, not living long enough to see the war's conclusion, the programs he initiated before the war had commenced would stand as great bulwarks of support for returning veterans.

One of the most consequential was the Selective Service Act of 1940, which ensured that any Americans drafted into the armed forces and made to head overseas could immediately expect their jobs to be repatriated to them upon their return. This was an about-face from what the veterans of World War One had experienced. Most of the troops returning from World War One came back home and found themselves entirely shut out of their previous jobs and with very little opportunity to find another one.

President Roosevelt, who was elected an astonishing four times (this was prior to term limits being set), was a tremendous planner. This was evidenced in July 1943 when he gave a radio address (one of his famed fireside chats) to the American public in which he specifically outlined his plans to aid returning veterans.

Roosevelt spoke, "While concentrating on military victory, we are not neglecting the planning of things to come. Among many other things we are, today, laying plans for the return to civilian life of our gallant men and women of the armed services. They must not be demobilized into an environment of inflation and unemployment. We must, this time, have plans ready—instead of waiting to do a hasty, inefficient, and ill-considered job at the last moment."

Since Roosevelt's 1944 reelection bid loomed, one could mark all this off as part of a campaign speech. But even so, Roosevelt followed through with his words and made sure that solid programs were in place to aid veterans. In 1944, FDR enacted the Serviceman's Readjustment Act. This was the bill that would become known as the G.I. Bill of Rights and later just the G.I. Bill.

As mentioned, this bill ensured college tuition would be paid, but that was only one benefit it provided. It also gave vets as much as fifty-two weeks of unemployment compensation and loans to purchase homes. Of course, then as is now, whenever big government spending is executed, there were critics of the initiatives. As nice as they sounded, there were those who openly wondered how the federal government would pay for all of it.

The Wall Street Journal even went as far as to lambast the measures as "a halfway house to socialism." In reality, much of the success of these programs was due to the dominant position the United States took immediately after the war.

At the end of World War One, the US was still just a regional power, dwarfed by Great Britain. After World War Two, these roles were reversed. The United States emerged as the greatest military and industrial powerhouse on the planet, while Britain was in severe distress, struggling to hang onto its crumbling empire.

The post-war boom of the United States was real, and the American dollar soon became an even greater asset than the American military. American currency was largely responsible for rebuilding bombed-out western Europe. Through the Marshall Plan, the US sought to restore stability in Europe, preventing Soviet infiltration by bolstering Europe's infrastructure. The same rebuilding project was also carried out in post-war American-occupied Japan.

Economic success and military might would be needed when the ideology of capitalism and free enterprise went head-to-head with the ideology of communism and state planning. The Cold War loomed large between the United States and Soviet Russia.

Chapter 11: The Cold War Challenges (1945-1990)

"The soldier above all others prays for peace. For it is the soldier who must suffer and bear the deepest wounds and scars of war."
-Douglas MacArthur

The Cold War between the United States of America and the Soviet Union began just about as soon as the guns of World War Two stopped firing. Although the Americans and the Soviets were allies during the war, they were ideologically mismatched from the beginning. The former Russian Empire had transformed itself into a communist state known as the Soviet Union (the USSR) back in 1917. The drama of World War One instigated this transformation.

By the time of World War Two, the US and the Soviet Union were unlikely allies, forging bonds together more out of necessity than anything else. They had common foes to fight and threw in their lots to dispatch them. However, after the war, all bets were off.

Most of the engagements of the Cold War presented themselves as a chess match of proxy wars. The Greek Civil War of 1946, the ideological struggle in Cuba in the 1960s, and the battle for Angola in the 1980s were all part of the larger Cold War, with one proxy set against another. Nations were either in the pro-Western capitalist camp or the pro-Soviet communist camp.

There were some fairly "hot" wars during this struggle, such as the ones in Korea and Vietnam. Both of these wars created serious consternation in America and on the world stage. The Korean War was a fairly straightforward matter. Korea was annexed by the Japanese back in 1910. With Japan's defeat in 1945, the Japanese lost control of the Korean Peninsula, and Korean independence was restored.

However, this independence came at a cost since the peninsula ended up being split along the 38th parallel, with the Soviets backing a communist government in the north and America and its allies backing a capitalist/democratic government in the south. This agreement was first proposed at the Potsdam Conference in July of 1945, just prior to Japan's defeat.

The splitting of the nation was to be temporary, as the newly freed Korea was allowed to decide what form of government it would like to have. The referendum on the fate of the Korean Peninsula never happened, though. The North Koreans rejected overtures by the United Nations to hold a referendum on the matter in 1948. The South Koreans went ahead and forged their own independent republic with the full blessing of the UN, electing their first official president, Syngman Rhee.

President Rhee would be crucial in the defense of South Korea, as he supported the Republic of Korea Army (ROKA for short). The ROKA would hold off North Korean aggression just long enough to enable US and UN forces to intervene. This intervention was needed after June 25th, 1950, when North Korean troops backed by the Soviet Union stormed across the 38th parallel and launched an assault on South Korea.

The cause of the Korean War should be fairly clear. North Korea wanted to unite all of Korea under a communist government, but South Korea wanted to keep its democracy intact. So, the North Koreans had to unite the peninsula under the communist banner by force. They crossed over the parallel and launched an invasion.

It is interesting to think what things might have been like if the US did not ultimately drive the North Koreans back. There would likely be no such thing as Samsung phones and Kia cars if the capitalist South Korean government had been toppled. Such a statement probably seems a bit ridiculous in light of all of the lives lost to keep the status quo of a half-communist/half-capitalist Korea. Plus, much more was at stake than the future of Samsung phones.

In the zero-sum game of the Cold War, it was feared that if a capitalist government fell to communism, it would create a domino effect in which more capitalist governments would fall. The United States feared that if they failed to protect South Korea, Japan might be next.

From the safety of more secure times, we might be tempted to believe that such fears were overblown. But from the perch of the immediate post-war world, these fears were very real concerns.

At the outset of the invasion, the US presence had dwindled down to no more than some five hundred military advisors, who were ostensibly in place just to bolster and train the nascent South Korean forces. As North Korean troops poured into the south, these few hundred American service members faced a dire fate should the South Korean army entirely collapse.

Fortunately for them, the South Korean defenses held long enough for reinforcements to arrive. The North Korean invasion of South Korea was, in many ways, the first real test of the United Nations. The United Nations had been established in the aftermath of World War Two in an attempt to create an international body that could mediate and solve disputes that might otherwise lead to armed conflict. When North Koreans ran roughshod over South Korea, the UN realized they had to act to demonstrate to the world that North Korea was in clear violation of the protocols the UN had established.

Even so, US President Harry S. Truman was loath to declare war. Initially, he leaned on the agency of the United Nations to face the threat of the North Koreans. The UN immediately demanded that the invasion cease, and when this obviously was not going to happen, it began to mobilize military support for the ROKA forces. Along with UN support, the United States authorized troops to be sent from nearby Japan.

The United States had placed Japan under direct military occupation since the end of the Second World War in 1945. A total of three divisions were rushed over from Japan to South Korea. These troops were still not quite adequate enough to stem the tide of the North Koreans. And during the first few weeks of their deployment, they were severely bruised and battered by the relentless

North Korean offensive.

Progress was not made until the following month of August, when the US and South Korean troops were able to reposition themselves well enough to halt the North Korean advance. More importantly, an experienced field commander and tactician, Lieutenant General Walton H. Walker, came onto the scene and directed the deployment of precious war materiel, such as rocket launchers, artillery pieces, anti-aircraft guns, and even tanks. He also coordinated with the US Air Force to generate effective air cover from above.

The United States Air Force was relatively new at that point. The US didn't even have an air force during World War Two, although it still flew planes in the war. In 1947, the US Air Force was officially established. And the cutting-edge Sabre jets that soared above Korea were much more advanced than the propeller-driven Mustangs the US operated during World War Two.

All of these measures were decisive in preventing the complete collapse of South Korea. The US Air Force, in particular, was pivotal, as it threw just about everything it had into the fray. From the old, aforementioned P-51 Mustangs to more advanced jet fighters, the US Air Force made sure that it dominated the skies over the Korean Peninsula. Also of use was a bolstered South Korean force that was able to double its size by recruiting its reserve troops and student volunteers.

From the very beginning, the South Koreans' enthusiasm to repel the North Koreans was much more robust in comparison to the lackluster performance of the South Vietnamese against the North Vietnamese, something we will talk about in more detail shortly.

At any rate, once the front line of defense was stabilized, General Douglas MacArthur looked toward launching a counteroffensive. He believed that the best way to do so would be to launch an amphibious landing behind the North Korean positions. This operation was executed on September 14th, 1950, when US Marines unleashed an assault on Wolmi Island.

The following day, US forces marched on Inchon, which they used as a forward base to reach Seoul by September 25th. On September 26th, General MacArthur and South Korean President Syngman Rhee stepped inside the capital complex and announced that South Korea had been liberated. However, being liberated and defeating the North

Koreans would quickly prove to mean two different things.

Although the North Korean forces had been greatly degraded, they had not been entirely defeated. Immediately after the South Koreans retook Seoul, some twenty-five thousand North Korean troops repositioned themselves in the mountainous regions farther north, where they waited to regroup. The North Korean troops wreaked much havoc as they fled, killing thousands of civilians in what was nothing but blatant war crimes. Both sides committed war crimes in the war, including the Americans. War remains a bloody affair to this day, and it is safe to say that, for the most part, no side is entirely innocent when it comes to bloodshed.

At this point, there was a plan to march north of the parallel and knock out the North Korean government completely to facilitate the unification of a capitalist-friendly Korean Peninsula. On October 7th, the plans were approved by the UN General Assembly, with the caveat that a larger war with China or Russia must be avoided at all costs. US troops began marching over the 38th parallel shortly afterward.

The core that remained of the North Korean Army, as well as the North Korean government itself, sought refuge near the Yalu River across from the Chinese border. The North Koreans might have seemed beaten, but really, they were just waiting for a massive avalanche of Chinese troops. China's leader, Chairman Mao Zedong, answered North Korea's call for support, which had been requested by the North Korean leader, Kim Il-Sung.

Mao was initially hesitant, but after Joseph Stalin assured him that Soviet airpower would ensure that bases and industrial plants on the Chinese side of the Yalu River would be protected, he mobilized Chinese forces to cross into North Korea and join the fray. This force was led by General Peng Dehuai, a hardened and battle-tested general who fought off both the Japanese during World War Two and the Chinese Nationalists during the Chinese Civil War, the war that precipitated China's inauguration as a communist nation.

General Peng Dehuai led the Chinese First Offensive on October 25th, 1950, which lasted until November 6th, 1950. During this military operation, the US and ROKA positions were mercilessly battered, and a total of seven US and South Korean regiments were wiped out. The Chinese also suffered heavy losses in the process, with some ten thousand dead troops in the aftermath. This first foray was, more or less, a test of the Americans' and South Koreans' resolve.

General Peng Dehuai took note of how the battle played out and determined that the best strategy moving forward would be to launch sudden surprise attacks, block supply routes, pull back, and then launch another sneak attack against the anticipated American/South Korean counterattack. The Americans and South Koreans had no choice but to pull back, regrouping south of the Ch'ongch'on River.

MacArthur made a near-fatal mistake on November 24th when he attempted to send the 8th Army and the X Corps farther north. The Chinese suddenly launched a ferocious attack and nearly split the army in half. The troops counterattacked and pulled a victory from what seemed like a certain defeat, but it was a costly engagement. Even worse, the Chinese were now emboldened and began pushing farther south.

Their aim had expanded to not just seeking to get the Americans out of North Korea but also to drive them off the Korean Peninsula itself. With this grand objective in mind, the Chinese Third Offensive was launched on December 31st, 1950. The offensive would last until January 5th, 1951, and would result in a communist victory that saw the Americans and their allies driven out of Seoul.

The Chinese and North Koreans were back in control of the South Korean capital and looked to take over the entire Korean Peninsula. Desperate to roll this relentless offensive back, United Nations forces were tapped, which brought new recruits to the conflict. These recruits hailed from a wide variety of UN member states. Incredibly enough, troops from Turkey, France, Belgium, Greece, Colombia, Ethiopia, Thailand, the Philippines, and Holland all saw action. The bolstered forces were able to hit back at their opponents, but it was slow-going.

In the meantime, US President Harry S. Truman had become entirely disenchanted with Douglas MacArthur's leadership and dismissed him from the war. General Matthew Ridgway would now be the top boss as it pertained to US forces in Korea. The allied forces led by the United States were able to rally, and by May, they were crossing back over the 38th parallel as the Chinese and North Koreans were once again pushed back.

By June 1951, both sides were drawn into peace talks due to

significant casualties. Interestingly, both sides had lost the will to unify Korea and sought to reestablish the status quo of a communist north and a capitalist south. Mao also had some political chicanery of his own in mind. He realized that if he were involved in the peace process as a big player standing toe to toe with the United States, it would, without a doubt, catapult China as the most powerful player in East Asia.

As hard as it might have been for Western minds to comprehend, this was very important to the Chinese, who wished to send a message to Japan, their former enemy. The Japanese had sought to dominate East Asia and waged terrible wars of aggression against China, Korea, and much of the rest of Southeast Asia. Japan was militarily defeated in World War Two, and many Chinese believe Japan was then *politically* defeated in the aftermath of the Korean War, which saw China elevated to the top of the world stage.

Although the Soviet Union had been the instigator of the conflict, it quietly voiced its assent to a return to the status quo in Korea. And in the end, that is what happened. After all of the bloodshed, Korea reverted back to the status it held before the Korean War began, with the North and the South definitively separated at the 38th parallel, with the hostilities coming to a close in 1953. By then, the United States had elected a new president, Dwight D. Eisenhower, who ran on a pledge to end fighting in Korea.

Considering the fact that both North Korea and South Korea ended up back where they had started, it is mind-boggling to consider the casualties. Nearly five million souls lost their lives just to revert back to the status quo. Around 2.5 million North Koreans (civilians and soldiers) are estimated to have perished, while 1.3 million South Koreans (civilians and soldiers) were killed. The death toll of US troops was much lower at around thirty-seven thousand, but even so, that is a daunting number all the same. And, of course, one death is one too many as far as the loved ones of any soldier are concerned.

And all of this for what? A return to the same old? Well, as silly as it might seem for so much bloodshed, there were many Cold War soldiers and officers who would insist that it was indeed worth it. US military strategists believed the loss of South Korea would have been unthinkable, so the mere fact that South Korea was preserved was considered a triumph.

The same thing could be said of the communists. To communist leaders, the loss of the communist enclave of North Korea would have been equally intolerable. Communists would have been much dismayed to have a thriving capitalist US-backed state right on the borders of communist China. For them, the buffer zone of having a communist North Korea was worth all the blood in the world.

Yes, it is hard for many of us today to understand the Cold War mindset that led to such outlooks, but it is important to view such things as the people back then would. And soon after the Korean War was over, US military strategists looked at the fields of Vietnam with horror.

Vietnam had been a French colony until the Japanese shook the French grip loose in World War Two. Communist insurgents holed up in the north and, under a charismatic leader by the name of Ho Chi Minh, staged a resistance against the Japanese. The communists of North Vietnam were even tacitly supported by the Allies since the "any enemy of my enemy is my friend" attitude had prevailed. Yet when Japan surrendered any claim to Vietnam in 1945, there was no seat at the table for the communists.

Even so, Ho Chi Minh and his cohorts were willing to take matters into their own hands, staging a revolt against the French, who had come to reclaim their territory. Ho Chi Minh and his men even briefly took over Hanoi. The French, with the aid of the British and, incredibly enough, some remaining Japanese, were able to fight off the insurgency, enabling the French to reclaim their role as colonial overlords. But it would not last. As soon as the North Vietnamese communists were able to regroup, they launched a bitter war against the French forces from their stronghold in the north.

The French were severely weakened by World War Two, and they were all but defeated by the North Vietnamese communists in 1954. Although communist and capitalist ideologies would be at the center of the later conflict, initially, the North Vietnamese could be considered part of a longer struggle against French colonialism. Many Vietnamese who rallied under the North Vietnamese banner saw communism as a convenient vehicle to use to throw off the French yoke.

The United States saw all of this strictly through the lens of the Cold War. It could have cared less about French colonial ambitions but was deeply concerned that if the communist North Vietnamese seized the whole of Vietnam and even the rest of what was then termed Indochina, all of Southeast Asia could be next. The Americans felt that if South Vietnam fell, then Laos and Cambodia would not be far behind.

Shortly after the French faced defeat in 1954, American military advisors began pouring into South Vietnam. The Americans initially wanted to serve in an advisory capacity and bolster the strength of the South Vietnamese armed forces. It was not until 1965, under the Lyndon B. Johnson administration, that things began to heat up, with actual combat troops being quietly introduced into the region. And by 1969, some 500,000 US troops were in Vietnam at any given time. The Americans hoped to stave off a South Vietnamese collapse with their large numbers.

At the same time this was going on, the Soviet Union and China were placing their own advisors in the region. Weapons and supplies also freely flowed from the communist bloc. The Soviets also gifted the North Vietnamese with Mig Jetfighters. This pipeline of technical support and supplies all but ensured that the Vietnam War would be a bloody one.

The political and social climate of Vietnam was also much different from Korea. While the South Koreans generally liked their leadership and government, the South Vietnamese were essentially ruled by a US-backed dictator and grew to despise their own governance. As such, the will to fight the North was incredibly low. Even worse, communist insurgents known as the National Liberation Front of South Vietnam, more commonly known as the Viet Cong, became a real thorn in the side of US troops to the point that the Americans often did not know who they could trust on the ground.

A South Vietnamese villager might seem friendly one moment and then open fire on US troops the next. This was the daily dilemma that US troops faced in South Vietnam. And as unpopular as the efforts to prop up South Vietnam might have been among the South Vietnamese, it became even more unpopular in the United States. The Vietnam War kicked off a series of popular protest movements in which the youth culture of America loudly demanded an end to all fighting in Vietnam.

The resistance in South Vietnam proved fatal in the overall war effort, as a vast pipeline of supplies from the northern communists to the Viet Cong, known as the Ho Chi Minh Trail, would keep the Viet Cong in the south well supplied. The United States tried to shut the trail down but was never quite able to do so. And as US troops and their allies became boxed in by insurgents in the north and south, the war was increasingly seen as a lost cause.

By the time of Richard Nixon's presidency, talk of ending the war became a paramount part of US policy. Winning the war was no longer on the agenda; instead, the US just wanted to end it. Nixon sought to find the best possible exit and dubbed the efforts to bring an end to hostilities "peace with honor." These efforts outlived Nixon, who resigned in 1974. His successor, Gerald Ford, would end US involvement in Vietnam on April 30th, 1975, which was when the last Americans left.

The United States had worked out a plan for withdrawal that would have kept the North Vietnamese at bay until the US troops were out, but things did not go quite so smoothly. When the US began to pull out, the North Vietnamese poured in, leading to terrible scenes of evacuation helicopters filled to the brim with civilians fleeing from the roofs of buildings as the capital of South Vietnam, Saigon, fell to communist forces.

As important as Korea and Vietnam were, they were not the only flash points of the war. West and East Germany are another great example. Germany, just like Korea and Vietnam, found itself divided between a communist and a capitalist government. Unlike Korea and Vietnam, the reunification of Germany, which was achieved shortly after the fall of the Berlin Wall, was a largely peaceful event.

East Germany was in dire economic straits, and West Germany was flourishing. The East Germans demanded a better life for themselves and the dismantling of the infamous Berlin Wall. That wall came down without a shot being fired on November 9th, 1989. The unification of Germany was a surprisingly speedy process, with unification being completed on October 3rd, 1990. Shortly thereafter, most of the old communist bloc became undone with the dissolution of the Soviet Union on December 26th, 1991.

Ironically enough, with the exception of Cuba, the feared dominoes in Asia would remain the only communist bulwarks. After the communist regimes collapsed in Europe, China, Vietnam, and

North Korea remained firmly locked in the grip of communism.

The Cold War would leave behind the terrible legacy of huge stockpiles of nuclear weapons. At the end of the Cold War, the US had a stockpile of around twenty-three thousand nuclear weapons, whereas the Soviet Union had around thirty-nine thousand. China had amassed over two hundred, and Britain and France had around five hundred each. Any one of these stockpiles would have been more than enough to destroy the planet.

The ridiculousness of such an arsenal was clear to most by the end of the Cold War, and concrete efforts (most notably with the former Soviet Union) were made to reduce nuclear arms. By 2020, the US and the Soviet Union's successor state—the Russian Federation—were roughly on par, with around six thousand nuclear weapons each. It seems that the Cold War concept of mutually assured destruction and the utter futility of nuclear weapons is at least one lesson of the Cold War that has been learned well.

Chapter 12: Post-Cold War (1990–2001) and the 21st Century (2001–2021) Conflicts

"Although a soldier by profession, I have never felt any sort of fondness for war. And I have never advocated it, except as a means of peace."

-*Ulysses S. Grant*

Much of the world breathed a sigh of relief with the collapse of the old communist bloc and the end of the Cold War. The long-standing conflict had pitted ideologies and nuclear-tipped missiles, but thankfully, the world did not have to undergo World War Three. But in the aftermath of the Cold War, many wondered what shape the post-war order would take.

For decades, someone was either in the Soviet-backed communist camp or the American-backed capitalist camp. But this worldview ended once communist domination in Eastern Europe fell. Instead of everything revolving around whether one was a communist or a capitalist, the US had to consider other concerns. And the first war to break out in this new world order had nothing to do with capitalism or communism.

Iraqi dictator Saddam Hussein invaded Kuwait, and the US decided to put boots on the ground in the Gulf War. This military operation was launched not to stave off a communist advance but to keep Saddam's hands off of Kuwait. Iraq was still reeling in the aftermath of the devastating Iran-Iraq War that raged from 1980 to 1988 and accomplished very little, except to send Iraq into deep debt.

And two of Iraq's major creditors at the time were the oil-rich countries of Saudi Arabia and Kuwait, which loaned Iraq substantial sums of money. At the end of the Iran-Iraq War, cash-strapped Iraq was unable to pay. Instead of paying up, Saddam, who cited the historical fact that Kuwait was once a part of Iraq, decided to invade Kuwait instead.

The United Nations gave Saddam a timeline to withdraw, and when he refused, the United States created a coalition to stand up to Iraq's aggression. The Americans and their allies were successful in this effort, and the conflict seemed to further demonstrate to the world America's clear and decisive military capabilities.

During this conflict, the US first used stealth aircraft, which rendered Saddam's radar stations useless. US planes were able to fly over Iraq with impunity. And by mid-January of 1991, the Iraqi Air Force had been completely obliterated. The US Army continued to make rapid gains, and Kuwait was liberated on February 25th, 1991. The rapid pace of the US-led victory in Iraq shocked the world and seemed to indicate the establishment of the new post-Cold War order, one in which the United States had unquestioned dominance.

By the end of the decade, specters of the Cold War raised their head with the eruption of the Kosovo War in 1998. This conflict erupted over the remnants of former Yugoslavia, which disintegrated shortly after the collapse of the Soviet Union in 1991.

But although the end of communism precipitated the splintering of Yugoslavia, much of the fighting was over much older fault lines in the region, such as religion and even ethnicity. The Kosovo War pitted Christians against Muslims. The US stepped into this fray with the intention of stopping the carnage and used the agency of what was essentially a relic of the Cold War—NATO—to halt the massacre that was taking place. Russia occasionally rattled its saber, as it did not appreciate a NATO intervention in its backyard. Nevertheless, NATO was able to secure peace.

Little did anyone know that a religious extremist group based out of Afghanistan was planning a catastrophic terrorist attack on the US mainland. The mastermind behind this plan was none other than Osama bin Laden.

Interestingly enough, bin Laden also had his roots in the Cold War. Bin Laden was not pro-capitalist or pro-communist, but he was backed by the American CIA as a militia leader. He led his Mujahideen. to battle the Soviet Union's troops, which had invaded Afghanistan in 1979. Although the Mujahideen could be considered an extremist outfit in just about every sense of the word, the mere fact they were fighting the Soviets made them temporary allies of the Americans. Bin Laden was a wealthy Saudi who traveled to Afghanistan with the sole desire of pushing the infidel Russians out.

After this was achieved, he quietly built up his following until he was confident that he could launch an attack on the Americans with whom he had previously been allied. Bin Laden's beef was not against communism. Instead, Osama bin Laden was a pure and simple religious extremist who wished to make Islam the most dominant religion on the planet.

And in his mind, the US, which had bases all over the Middle East and other traditionally Muslim lands, had to be pushed out. He issued a declaration declaring as much in 1996, but much of the world did not take it seriously. It was not until several hijacked planes hit US targets in New York and Washington, DC, on September 11th, 2001, causing tremendous death and destruction, that the world took notice. The War on Terror would begin in earnest.

Initially, the war had the limited scope of taking out bin Laden and al-Qaeda, a group of Islamic extremists who were based out of Afghanistan. This is the pure and simple logic that led to the War in Afghanistan, which would degrade al-Qaeda and their hosts, the Taliban. A large part of the relentless pounding of al-Qaeda and Taliban positions was done through drones equipped with offensive weaponry. Although such things are commonplace today, back in the early 2000s, this was cutting-edge technology.

As clear-cut as the operations were in this early phase of the War in Afghanistan, it was when the war spilled over to Iraq in 2003, the objectives of the War on Terror became much more obscure. The US launched strikes against Afghanistan with the intention of taking out al-Qaeda and the extremist Taliban who gave them safe haven. Such things were easily understood, but the push to invade Iraq was not.

There were claims that Saddam Hussein, the foe of the Gulf War, had weapons of mass destruction and was supporting terrorists. These claims were unfounded and ultimately proven to be untrue. Still, the US made the decision to invade, and as such, it was responsible for the invasion and the subsequent occupation after Saddam Hussein was toppled. US troops would not withdraw from Iraq until 2011.

Back over in Afghanistan, the fight against the Taliban continued all the way until 2021, when the US, under the leadership of President Joe Biden, executed a full withdrawal. The sudden withdrawal was highly controversial since it caught many US allies off-guard. Nevertheless, the US withdrawal of troops, which had been long in the making, was finally achieved.

However, it resulted in a complete Taliban takeover and the dismantling of a US-backed democratic government that had been in place for nearly twenty years. The Taliban have pledged to keep al-Qaeda from returning, but it is hard to say what the final objectives were at the end stage of the War on Terror.

Conclusion: The View from the Top

The US Armed Forces have gone through quite a number of changes during their steady evolution as the premiere fighting force on the planet. In the beginning, all America had was a ragtag bunch of militias cobbled together out of last-minute necessity. Soon after the Revolutionary War and especially after the War of 1812, regional militias were considered obsolete.

Militia forces were simply not adequate enough when it came to creating a unified front against large professional armies. The War of 1812 all but proved this to be the case. Military officers now received official training, and an established protocol of command had been developed. The US Army went from ragtag bands of fighting men to disciplined units. The army became utterly transformed by the time of the Mexican-American War and even more so by the outbreak of the American Civil War.

By the time of World War One, American troops were much better disciplined, and their procedures and protocol were more uniform. Still, the American military was, at best, a regional power and had great difficulty in projecting strength overseas. Sure, the US Armed Forces secured a victory against the weakened Spanish Empire in Cuba and the far-flung Philippines, but in comparison to other world powers, such as Britain and France, the US was not considered a competitor.

It was only in the aftermath of World War Two that the US rose to the occasion. Japan bombed Pearl Harbor, hoping to knock the US out of the war but instead woke a sleeping giant. The US military and US industry kicked into high gear and began churning out troops, aircraft, naval vessels, and tanks like there was no tomorrow. Neither the Japanese, the Italians, nor the Germans could keep up.

The Axis was doomed the second the US entered the war. And after the conclusion of World War Two, the US emerged as one of the most dominant players on the world stage, with that other player being the Soviet Union. With the Western and Eastern powers locked in an ideological standoff, the Cold War erupted.

The US came out on top of this challenge, becoming the dominant military force on the globe. But even so, the US faced many unforeseen threats.

The War on Terror challenged US dominance. The US had made it to the top, but would it be able to keep its place? The US is now seeking to keep the status quo, as renewed threats from both Russia and China have emerged in what is shaping up once again as a multipolar world of multiple power players. It is still unclear what the future might hold, but rest assured, the enduring strength of the US military will play a part in it.

Here's another book by Captivating History that you might like

Free Bonus from Captivating History (Available for a Limited time)

Hi History Lovers!

Now you have a chance to join our exclusive history list so you can get your first history ebook for free as well as discounts and a potential to get more history books for free! Simply visit the link below to join.

Captivatinghistory.com/ebook

Also, make sure to follow us on Facebook, Twitter and Youtube by searching for Captivating History.

Appendix A: Further Reading and Reference

Atkinson, Rick. *The British Are Coming: The War for America, Lexington to Princeton, 1775-1777.* 2019.

Bellesiles, A. Michael. *A People's History of the U.S. Ordinary Soldiers Reflect on Their Experiences of War, from the American Revolution to Afghanistan.* 2013.

Gilbert, Martin. *The First World War: A Complete History.* 1965.

Hosch, L. William. *The Korean War and the Vietnam War: People, Politics, and Power.* 2009.

Made in the USA
Monee, IL
25 November 2023